Articles assembled and edited here have
earlier appeared in the following columns,
blogs and magazines: *New Swirled Order*
in *The Cerealogist*, edited by John Michell;
Cornography in *SC Magazine*, formerly *Sussex
Circular*, edited by Andy Thomas; *The Voice of
Reason* in *www.swirlednews.com*, also edited by
Andy Thomas; and *The Wheat from the Chaff* in
www.michaelglickman.net.

Cornography - The New Swirled Order
first published 2007 AD
© Michael Glickman 2007 AD

Published by The Squeeze Press.
8A Market Place, Glastonbury, Somerset

British Library Cataloguing in Publication Data
Glickman, M.
Cornography: Despatches from the Crop Circles

A CIP catalogue record for this little book
is available from the British Library

ISBN10   1 906069 04 2
ISBN13   978 1 906069 04 9

Printed on Forestry Stewardship Council approved
paper from sustainably managed forests.

Printed and bound in Great Britain
by The Cromwell Press,
Trowbridge, Wiltshire, UK.

the
SQUEEZE
PRESS

DESPATCHES FROM THE CROP CIRCLES

CORNOGRAPHY

THE NEW SWIRLED ORDER

Michael Glickman

to my many friends and colleagues

in the crop circle world

who have the courage and grace

to admit that they simply do not know

CONTENTS

INTRODUCTION

Some years ago I spent a weekend with John Martineau and his family on the Welsh borders. On the first night, I found that I had been thoughtfully provided with some bedtime reading. A small pile of *Sussex Circulars* was on the bedside table. Certainly, I had heard rumours about this little magazine but had never read it. I stayed awake for hours and was bleary-eyed at breakfast.

I had been aware of, and curious about, these strange circular marks for a while before the arrival of the enormous and enigmatic Alton Barnes pictogram in July of 1990. This was the first formation I visited and I suppose I never got out. Just a few weeks later I was honoured when John Michell invited me to write a regular column for *The Cerealogist*. The journal was still in its infancy but the portents were good; the only editorial line in evidence was a rigorous openness, and its serious intent had not precluded wit. Though flattered, I protested to John "But I know nothing about crop circles". "Exactly, my dear" he replied.

I wrote *New Swirled Order* for three astonishing years. Michell's editorship was open, inspiring and exemplary. It was a radiant time. But the shadows of the Doug and Dave hoax scam were growing longer and were to damage crop circle research and many of its leading heroes irrevocably. John Michell, I think, sensed this and relinquished his editorship at what was, probably, the perfect time. I managed to hang on for one more issue but then, guiltily (a rat leaving a sinking ship), I too deserted.

My first readings of *The Sussex Circular* in the small hours of dawn in that tiny guest bedroom were reassuring. Here was a little publication – a light at the end of a tunnel – without pomposity or pretension which observed, lightly and reasonably, the strangeness which absorbed more and more of my conscious time. Inevitably after a while I took out a subscription and – equally inevitably – I started a telephone relationship with the editor, Andy Thomas. Finally – to my real satisfaction – I was offered a column – *Cornography*.

Many of us have had our lives, if not changed, then certainly modified by these extraordinary occurrences. There can be few experiences as moving and joyful as a visit to a circle; I hope my scribblings, compiled and edited here into more of a modern blog, can echo some of the curiosity, excitement and anticipation that many of us have felt as these beautiful events unfold.

3

4

A Wiltshire correspondent writes:

7:00 am

Once again I awake to the sound of those confounded helicopters. Why they have to practice their static hovering so low over the cornfields is beyond me. I have complained to the police, but they claim to know nothing about it. Meanwhile the number of helicopters seems to increase every week.

10:20 am

At work I glance through the window and see, to my astonishment, a man clambering into the back garden, followed by several others. I rush out to find a similar party climbing in over the opposite wall. They are all carrying rods and sticks and, it appears, had been following two important "ley" lines which, I am excitedly though incoherently informed, intersect in the area of my azaleas. A major "pictogram" is to appear on my back lawn. It seems appropriate to give them coffee.

There are eleven of them.

12:45 pm

A light lunch disturbed by screeching of tyres and ringing of door bell. A Japanese television crew, in two substantial vehicles, wishes to record the manifestation of the "pictogram"! Bowing, they ask permission to set up their equipment in the garden. I feel it would be churlish to refuse, though the cables through my study are an irritation.

3:15 pm

On the way to collect Emily from school I see the Army in the fields yet again. As always they are lying perfectly still in the corn waiting for darkness and pretending they are not there. Someone should tell them that the sand-coloured desert kit (though clearly better than khaki drab) stands out a mile. Also, their aluminium poles and elaborate ladders flash and glitter in the sunlight.

3:45 pm

Returning home, Emily cries out "Daddy, Daddy, look at all those deer. What are they doing to each other?" I don't feel up to explaining rutting so I tell her they are playing a game. I must say there are a lot of them and they do form perfect circles.

8:30 pm

Emily asleep and the Japanese standing stoically by their floodlights, I decide to go out for a drink. The pub is completely packed with drunken journalists, American photographers and Dutch hippies. Can't get into the snug. The landlord tells me a lady is doing a public "channelling" in there.

9:00

The Young Farmers arrive with their planks and coils of rope. They are arguing noisily about whether it should have been clockwise or anti-clockwise. It looks as though they will come to blows. I leave in disgust.

9:12

About a mile from home when the car is bathed in bright blue light and the electrics go out. I open the sun roof and give them the sharp edge of my tongue. "What is wrong with you people?" I scream up at them. "You've examined me already. Is there nobody up there who can keep proper records?" They sulk for a moment and then, putting what passes for their foot hard down, they whizz away and dematerialise.

9:25

Television team rather the worse for wear. Sake has been introduced into my living room. Refusing offers to see pictures of events in rice-fields, I go to my room.

10:00 pm

Drifting off to sleep despite tuneless rendition of "My Way" by camera crew downstairs. What is channelling? What is a pictogram? What is dowsing? What is going on?

* * * * *

Mr. Cyril Ardrossan of Worthing argues that the circles have been building to reach their peak this year – 1991 – in response to its being a palindrome. The last palindromic year was 1881 and, though he has no evidence, he firmly believes that circles must have appeared then. 1991 and 1881 are separated by 110 years and Mr. Ardrossan demonstrates the recurring similarity between the crop events and the graphic symbols 1, 8, 9, & 0.

The next palindromic year will be 2002 (a mere 11 years away) and Ardrossan is excited by the additional graphic possibilities offered by the number 2. According to his Palindromic Year Crop

Circles Hypothesis, the very crescendo of activity will be on the 1st of September (1 9 1991), probably at 9 minutes past 1 in the morning. Readers with information on 1881 crop circles should send it to me to be forwarded to Worthing.

* * * * *

Those, and there are many, who contend that the Crop Circles transform their students in an inexplicable but benign way, would have found a confirmation at the Cornference in Glastonbury. The occasion was entirely joyful.

The organisers had been concerned that the event would be under subscribed, but within an hour of the doors opening on the Saturday morning, people were having to be turned away. This popularity produced the only criticism of the meeting; the September weekend was warm and the otherwise perfect Assembly Rooms soon resembled a steam chamber.

It was worth braving the Turkish Bath. The programme offered an exhilarating mix of information, speculation and entertainment and for those who could not take the heat, the Cornference spilled into the streets and cafes of Glastonbury.

The programme was too extensive to review entirely, but, though any selection might be invidious, I hope I will be excused for mentioning two or three contributions.

The Sunday Lecture, 'Breaking the code of the Agriglyphs' was a prodigious piece of research which suggested a connection between the circles and the civilisation of Atlantis. Another speaker reported the detailed underlay construction of the circles. Like a Kiowa Apache tracker, he spends hours on his hands and knees, unravelling mysteries by the study of detail,

A teacher sang if not the only, then certainly the first crop circle song at the Corncert, the entertainment on Saturday evening. Though he made no other contribution to the Cornference his influence was pervasive. His work through the season to produce beautiful and accurate survey drawings as events occurred has helped us all in our attempts to start to unravel the meaning of this phenomenon.

* * * * *

It was ironic that the Doug & Dave "We-faked-all-the-circles" hoax hit the streets the very day after the Cornference. Those of us who had heard the crop circle godfathers speaking so sincerely and enthusiastically on the previous Saturday were shocked by what we read on the front page of *Today*.

For my part, having turned-on several American friends to the phenomenon, I was called at unearthly hours after the "news" hit the US. My friends were disillusioned. I felt like some awful dope dealer who had inexplicably shut off his clients' supplies. I reassured them they did not have to face cold turkey. Doug & Dave were liars and there would be more (real) circles next season.

Some months later, two interesting facts remain. First, there is no evidence that Doug & Dave produced a single circle, other than the rough simulacra carried out in the presence of the press. Second, the widespread, almost gleeful, acceptance of their claims says more about society's need to deny than about the hoax itself.

In this respect, D & D might be seen as an essential part of the development of the Crop Circles and they, or others like them, will probably continue – with more or less success – to hoax or claim to hoax. They will serve to remind us of our inherent need to deny the inexplicable.

* * * * *

As a part of the media circus for which this hoax scam was developed, Granada TV staged an audience-participation confrontation between, on the one side the con-men, Doug & Dave, and on the other an array of crop circle veterans. Of course, the barely concealed sub-text of this programme was "get the experts", that unpleasant side of our national character which reviles ideas and prides itself on its ability to belittle and debunk.

The idea that two "ordinary blokes", "artists" as *Today* suggested, men "of average intelligence" as they themselves claimed (though this latter is an assertion which – having seen them – I would dispute) might pull the rug on silly "experts" by a simple hoax, was supposed to have the audience screaming for the experts' blood. In fact, the audience (apart from the predictable token aggressive scientist) were restrained and reasonable. They offered little support for Doug & Dave.

Simply, they are self-confessed vandals, The National Farmers' Union should have sued them for damage to the several hundred fields they claimed.

* * * * *

I write some weeks before Christmas. It is four months since the appearance of the majestic Barbury Castle formation and somewhat less since the Mandelbrot and the "Brain".

In this breathing space everyone seems bemused. The events of the last season were so astonishing that many seem unable to contemplate a comparable step forward in 1992.

The suggestion was made at the Cornference that we should use this time to plan and design a mark of gratitude to the Circlemakers to be laid out, in a friendly farmer's field, at the start of the season. The reactive and humorous nature of the phenomenon asserts itself repeatedly. How would it react to a signal from us?

12

1992

Many students of the crop circle phenomenon have been anxious to discover where it goes in the winter time. I am pleased to say that I can now, exclusively, reveal the answer to this question.

This winter, the Circlemakers have shifted their attention to young men's heads! In the London area, an outbreak of strange geometric hair markings has caused bewilderment in dozens of families.

The Hair Circles, or Scalpoglyphs, obviously placed in a much smaller "field", have a delicacy of design comparable to the familiar crop events. However, the geometric and symbolic motifs are new and scalpologists are already surveying and measuring the patterns before they are destroyed by the next crop.

One authority suggests that the phenomenon is caused by the action of the air while drying the head, the "Hair Dryer Vortex Hypothesis"; this idea has been greeted with derision.

The owner of one formation, the "Palm Tree" (25th February 1992), refuses to give his name or address; he is worried that his head will be damaged by visitors. However he tells the following story which appears to be typical:

"I found myself in a strange steel and leather chair, a bit like a dentist's chair. The room was very bright and there were lots of mirrors.

A man stood behind me. He was dressed in white. He held my head in a vice-like grip. There was a powerful buzzing which seemed to go right into my head. I was frightened to move in case he hurt me. Then I was released into the street. These strange markings were all over my head!"

We will keep readers informed of further activity.

* * * * *

Like many of us, I lead an enforced double life. Many sections of the outside world are disturbed by mention of such things as crop circles. Your average bank manager, for instance, is not impressed to hear that his supposedly sober client spends obsessive hours with such marginal nonsense.

A year or so ago, my enthusiasm was uncontainable. It did not take too many glazed eyes and embarrassed silences to make me realise that, often, people preferred not to hear.

I travel a great deal and it has now become a rule for me never to raise the subject. Abroad, particularly, the risk of being taken as some kind of dingbat is high. Try convincing a dinner-party of solid Swiss manufacturers and their wives that the crop events have a spiritual nature!

But strange things happen. Last year, travelling through rural Ohio on the way to Dayton airport, my driver, a factory manager in shorts and baseball cap, asked, out of the blue, whether I knew anything about crop circles. He had been interested for months but had never discussed it with anyone.

A few months ago, in Australia at a business lunch, a woman who I had only just met asked me the same question. She, too, had felt increasingly interested in the phenomenon but had never spoken about it.

Inevitably I had material with me which I showed them and subsequently I sent them both books. In both case I asked them on what impulse they had raised the subject. They could not explain.

Have others had this experience? Do we croppies give off some kind of subliminal signal which identifies us to interested parties? An Agriglyph Pheromone perhaps?

* * * * *

The Annual General Meeting of the Centre for Crop Circle Studies (CCCS) in March left me bemused. It is a benign and affable organisation which, despite the best efforts of its excellent and devoted officers already shows signs of premature sclerosis. Perhaps this is in the nature of British organisations.

The real shock was the main speaker of the afternoon, a lady member of the Worshipful Company of Spectacle Makers. (Does that mean optician?) She certainly made a spectacle.

The speaker had obviously had a scientific training, for she felt confident in putting forward a hypothesis so dodgy that it made even unscientific cranks like me feel positively sane. Essentially, and insofar as I understood and can remember, certain emanations from the earth (energetic? radiant? gaseous? chemical?) were colliding with / impacting upon / reacting against / reflecting from military microwave transmissions and returning to earth to form the circles!

I was very proud of the way my fellow members restrained themselves. The Old Question was politely asked: If this is indeed the

Mechanism, how does it generate such particular Forms? Our speaker suggested that perhaps it was an elaborate joke. The British Army is well-known for its sense of humour, she claimed. Please! Military humour is to humour as military music is to music.

One of the delights of this phenomenon is that it provides an open and tolerant forum for speculation. The CCCS AGM, however, merits a rather more solid contribution.

* * * * *

I have a prediction for the coming season and I proposed giving it to a friend in a sealed envelope to be opened at the breathlessly awaited 1992 Cornference.

He would not have it. He made it clear that he would not play that kind of game. I should have the courage of my convictions and display it now.

I believe an ellipse will appear in July, at Barbury Castle. I have no idea of its size, but I believe the proportion will be about 1 to 1.77.

If it appears I will not be able to explain; if it does not, I will take the derision with fortitude.

* * * * *

The season is in full swing and I write this on the eve of *The Guardian* newspaper's Crop Circle Making Contest. The conditions have been published and include the figure to be constructed. My own feeling is that it is far too elaborate. The Circle Makers are not show-offs and have never included so many different motifs in a single event. Twelve teams, probably totalling over fifty participants, will attempt to duplicate this figure during five hours of darkness. If nothing else, this must be the largest physical response humanity has ever made to the phenomenon. Might it not have been – in its twelve repetitions – just a little more elegant? Could we not have responded to the Circlemakers with a form less shopping-list and more poetic?

Hopefully, a thirteenth plot will be left for our friends' reply.

* * * * *

I have just returned! The contest provided the best weekend I've had since last year's Cornference and I realise now how grouchy, nit-picking and ungracious my previous paragraph was. I withdraw it and apologise.

The event was a delight and the valiant teams performed prodigiously. Only in England could an enterprise so fundamentally surreal be carried off with such grace and style. It was pure fun.

I suspect that little has been learned. Those convinced that all crop circles are man-made will be comforted in that view by the excellence of the results we saw; those who feel that we are in the presence of angels, Gaia, fairies, aliens, lustful hedgehogs or species consciousness will find nothing here to change their mind.

* * * * *

I would like to solicit contributions from croppie poets. Odes or limericks, haikus or clerihews, sonnets or doggerel will all be considered for publication. Brevity is essential; ballads and epics will be cruelly and mindlessly cropped!

Our first contribution is from Mr. Ofmil C. Haynes (73) of Melton Mowbray.

Every year
More circles appear.
You'd think they would weary
Of each dingbat theory.

Hoax, alien or vortex.
No cerebral cortex
Can handle the synthesis
Of every hypothesis.
So, dear Cerealogist,
Don't turn explanologist!
Circles will accumulate
No matter how we speculate.

* * * * *

In the last issue of the *Cerealogist*, the result of the name vote was announced. There were 52 votes for *CereOlogist*, 16 for *CereAlogist* and, we are informed, 16 "deviants". I, dear reader, am proud to be one of those deviants. I wrote in formally to express the view that, to maintain the high standards of fairness to which the journal aspires, we had no alternative but to call it the *CerALOLOGIST*.

My letter was not published. Its overwhelmingly sensible suggestion was suppressed!

* * * * *

After the extraordinary events and enthusiasm of the last year's season it has been dispiriting to observe the extent to which this year's activities have been trivialised and damaged by hoax-fixation. Another fine mess we've got ourselves into.

Local groups have broken up, conferences have been distracted, senior figures have been humiliated, grown men have been seen to weep. And what for? Nobody can deny that certain glyphs were man-made but who cares? Only when it can be demonstrated that every single circle, in every country, is man-made will this utterly boring topic have any importance.

Why, then, does it exercise such morbid fascination for us? How have we allowed ourselves to become so bemused?

In the meantime, I have two suggestions. First, those who are obsessed by fakes, frauds and forgeries should set up the CFCCS, the Centre for Fake Crop Circle Studies or SCCP, the Society for Crop Circle Paranoiacs. We will give them all the support they need, provided they stay on their own turf. Second, and perhaps more practical, those of us who are interested in Crop Circles should undertake not to speak publicly or write about hoaxes. Deny them, to borrow a phrase, the oxygen of publicity. I took the oath myself at the Salisbury Cornference (though nobody joined me in it!) and consequently this will be my last word on this tedious subject!

This, I regret, is a promise I have made (and broken) many times during my Crop Circle years. I was so outraged by the blatant untruth of the hoax claims and the consistent untrustworthiness of the hoaxers, that I was unable to hold my tongue. In a way I regret it and yet, at some level, I am proud.

Meanwhile, those crop circle experts the Andrews Brothers, Colin and Richard, have been enticed to the United States by female CIA operatives where they are undergoing deep interrogation in secure houses outside Washington; the Mossad has set up a Crop Glyph fabrication camp in the Israeli Negev desert; agents of the Vatican are buying property in the Alton Barnes area; Mark Thatcher is selling second-hand crop circles to Saddam Hussein and, these pages can now reveal, the true purpose of George Wingfield's extended trip to America was to take part in secret negotiations with the UN Security Council.

21

1993

I suppose I remain very much a product of the '60s; an unreconstructed hippie. I suspect that I am not alone in relishing one of the incidental characteristics of the crop circle phenomenon – the tribalism.

Conferences, seminars and lectures become, year by year, more like ceremonial gatherings. Even visits to the circles, with their inevitable meetings and encounters, seem charged with a benign social significance.

The tribe is best observed at its summer gatherings where the elders, medicine men and wise women speak of the season's events. The young bring their reports from the fields and the soothsayers make their predictions.

The atmosphere is open and tolerant. For the good of the tribe, rivalries and disagreements are generously held in check.

* * * * *

There is, sadly, another aspect of these gatherings which seems to increase inexorably, year by year – the disease of chronic Guru-itis. Sufferers exhibit the following symptoms:

Symptom: Use of the royal plural. Delusions that they are a member of a wise and all-knowing team.

23

Cure: Ask loudly "Who are 'we'?"

Symptom: References to facts which are quickly glossed over or promised for "next year. "

Cure: Shout "Tell us NOW."

Symptom: Allusions to information given by channelers, Hopi Indians, entities, someone who knows a man in MI5.

Cure: Cry out "Just what did they actually SAY?"

Symptom: Use of phrases such as "I do assure you", "trust me" and "I wish I was in a position to share with you…"

Cure: Boo them off the platform.

This is another level of disinformation and one which we should not tolerate. Worse, this kind of half communication often masks incipient emotional breakdown. Sufferers should be treated with kindness and understanding.

* * * * *

I regret there was only one contribution to Poetry Circle and I must therefore assume that the readers of *The Cerealogist* are not poetically inclined. Perhaps a Croppie Problem Page might be more appropriate? Any personal dilemmas forwarded to me will be handled with sensitivity and discretion. I do assure you.

* * * * *

The Annual General Meeting of the CCCS kicked the season into play and, once again, members were bewildered by the keynote lecture presented in the afternoon. Last year's lecture by the lady spectacle-maker was so peculiar that many people were curious as to the motive behind management's choice.

This year our credulity was even further strained. Two gents wittered on for an hour, sharing the platform, and once again testing the audience to its limit. Simply, nobody understood what they were talking about!

I have given this some thought and I now understand the masterful strategy of the CCCS Council. They realise that, as the circles reappear, we will experience the inexplicable. They feel that, like some Zen initiation test, it will help prepare us if we have to suffer, at the start of each season, a totally meaningless and impenetrable presentation. Having understood this I am now filled with admiration for the performers of the last two years. How difficult it must be to plan and sustain incomprehensibility for so long.

The morning was devoted to the formal business of the CCCS, elections, accounts, budgets. Readers will know me to be a reasonable and unprovocative figure and so they will share my astonishment when I report that, after making a typically understated contribution, I was accused of being "messianic". I know that there has been some publicity about the large number of politicians, judges and particularly police officers involved in Messianic Lodges but this kind of thing has never appealed to me.

I had obviously made a mistake so I checked it in the dictionary.

"Messia'nic; a. Intelligent, astute, articulate, lucid; also very good looking." I stupidly had not understood and I would like to thank the lady at the AGM (whose name unfortunately I did not catch) for her compliment.

26

1994

My view is that our understanding of the Circles will increase at a pace established by their authors and no quicker. We should have learned by now that they will not be tricked or lured into disclosure. With this in mind I have been bemused and a little disturbed by news and communications from the USA.

A well-known Californian croppie wrote asking my help in a circle-making competition in oil-seed rape. I called him to thank him for his letter and to say, politely, that this was not my area of interest. He let me know, clearly, aggressively and at some length, that the only research of any value was being undertaken by his compatriots and the "`Brits" were all useless. This was followed by a further letter in much the same offensive tone.

And then at about the same time, a copy of a Crop Circle journal, published in America, was delivered. I was shocked to see the plan of the 1992 Silbury Charm Bracelet published above a copyright symbol and a name. Now, we all know that the bracelet was heroically surveyed at the eleventh hour by a team of enthusiasts. What is going on here? Attempting to claim a crop circle survey as personal intellectual property is rather like trying to patent an oak tree!

* * * * *

Jim Schnabel's much-rumoured book, *Round in Circles* has finally appeared, and what a nasty little effort it is. He sprays allegation and innuendo mindlessly at good and decent people, taking care (the coward) to steer just this side of libel, and producing not a shred of hard evidence to back up his fantasies. It tells us nothing about the circles but is a terrific read for those who wish to know more about young Jim's emotional freight.

* * * * *

Some time ago I referred to "the Andrews brothers, Colin and Richard" and their abduction by the CIA. This produced more mail than anything else I have ever written; people were very concerned to correct me. I must tell the truth; I knew they weren't brothers and, frankly, they have not really been spirited away by agents. It was supposed to be amusing.

Ah, well! It made Barbara and Beth, the Davis sisters, laugh. I do assure you!

* * * * *

The enthusiasm for the work of Dr. Levengood is entirely appropriate and the good Doctor must be applauded for his courage and persistence. For the first time, 'science' applied to the circles has been published in a peer review journal. This raises several issues. First, who are the 'peers' who review this work? Levengood is – I believe- almost alone in the scientific community in taking this subject seriously. I hope that he will be neither pilloried nor ignored; sadly, it is safe to predict that his work will not be widely celebrated and circulated.

Second, there is a tendency among croppies to see this kind of scientific work as some kind of talisman. If only we had scientific (or media) approval, they would not think we were crackpots anymore. This is dangerous ground. To pursue knowledge for its own value is unquestionably noble; to pursue it for some kind of social approval or redemption will only end in tears.

Third, Levengood's work, like that of all scientists, engages the tiniest (and, to me, least interesting) piece of the puzzle. Having seen Barbury Castle, Bythorn and the Avebury Spider's Web, I must confess that, though they overwhelm me with curiosity and awe, the mechanism by which the crop lies down is fairly low on my personal list of questions.

1995

I spent much of yesterday with my editor and a friend from California, Patricia Murray, in what was, we believe, one of the first circles of the season in the South of England. A small circle with two unusually wide rings in oilseed rape on a hillside within sight of the English Channel.

No doubt the formation will be reported in some detail soon. For my part, though I had been in rape formations before, I had never been in one on such a beautiful day when the crop was so high and so stridently yellow. We spent some time there; it was a delight.

Each of us took many photographs of the circle. The cameras all worked perfectly.... Here we go again!

* * * * *

I have been called a fanatical cultist, a zealot and similar mind-concentrating epithets because I find it hard to believe in hoaxes. Call me old fashioned, I just can't stretch my stolid, conservative mind around these new ideas. My grandmother could not explain them and what was good enough for her is certainly not going to be challenged by me.

These revolutionary ideas are distasteful and, above all, dangerous.

Just looking at the unappetising individuals who support these millennial notions – man-made indeed! – should be enough. Who would choose to belong to a team like that?

However, I must admit my faith was shaken earlier this year. I was lecturing in New York and CNN wanted to film the lecture and interview me and the audience. The reporter, Jean Moos, seeking background information, accessed the CNN news database (which one might imagine is reasonably comprehensive) only to find that, on the subject of crop circles, it had been severely edited, indeed scorched down. There were only two items left in the database – both about Doug & Dave. Now who in the world has the power to edit the CNN database and why would they ever want to?

Even I, bigot and fundamentalist that I am, thought for a moment that this might be evidence of a larger, high-level, orchestrated conspiracy. Thank goodness reason prevailed! The scorching of the database must have been a simple computer error. Of course. We can all go back to sleep.

* * * * *

The long-awaited London launch of a book on crop circle geometry was a wonderful event. Croppies came in from great distances. The Dreads came from Wiltshire, others from Petersfield, Stroud, Glastonbury and Southsea. The London contingent included various eminent philosophers and antiquarians

The point of this enterprise is the widespread take-up of geometric analysis in crop circle studies. It is now absolutely standard procedure that formations are checked this way.

There is a logic to this. Insofar as the crop circles could be said to have opened a conversation with us, it is a conversation in formal, geometric and mathematical terms. It is hardly surprising then that it responds so elegantly to formal and geometrical analysis.

* * * * *

Someone once called the human race "Information Harvesters". As poetic and charming as this phrase is, it leaves me with certain reservations. I guess the idea must have been conceived well before the electronic explosion; now, with the benefit of hindsight, we see how limited this idea might be. Would it not be better to belong to a race of "Wisdom Harvesters"?

I raise this because I see that, in crop circle circles, we seem unable to see the difference. If as many of us now accept, the phenomenon is drawing us towards something, I hope it will be wisdom rather than information.

The much-vaunted "scientific breakthrough", should it materialise, will be information rich and wisdom bankrupt.

* * * * *

Meanwhile, despite the reservations, it appears to me to be a very good start to the 1995 season. This is written at the end of June and we have already had the Nine Coil Spiral at Cherhill, the Quintuplet of Quintuplets at Cheesefoot Head and the beautiful Asteroid Belt at Alresford.

This is the kind of material we usually expect in July or August.

Are we having a whizzbang year or what?

* * * * *

As a general rule, it is safe to assume that 95 per cent does not exist. It has no reality and is never used seriously. It is an invented figure put forward with confidence by people who are desperate to make a point without any evidence.

We have seen two examples this year. I am told that a famous pop star asserted at the Cardiff UFO conference that 95% of circles this year were hoaxes and, on the Glastonbury Symposium coach tour, there were reports of a master dowser making the same claim.

Have they been speaking to each other? Do they know something we don't? Or is it that with not a shed of evidence, they reach for that reliable old talisman of sloppy thinking – 95%.

It only works, of course if it is pronounced with authority. The bubble bursts as soon as anyone asks "Why not 93. 75 or 96%" not to mention "How do you know?"

If they are correct, then of the eighty or so formations this year, only four are real. Perhaps these know-alls might share with us which they are?

* * * * *

That other great hoax apologist, Colin Andrews, arrived at Glastonbury to deliver our annual chastisement. He berates us, as usual, for our many inadequacies. Oh, it's true, it's true! What amazes me about the man is his acute vision. He arrives annually at the world's foremost crop circle gathering each year, attends not a single lecture, spends time with barely a single researcher, arrives ten minutes before and leaves ten minutes after his presentation, but STILL knows our failures and shortcomings.

I am sure we will all try to do better.

I hesitate to offer advice but perhaps it is time Colin was told that "phenomenon" is singular while "phenomena" is plural. As someone who makes his living from this phenomena he should be aware of it.

* * * * *

It was a curious season. The formations, though fewer, were of a great sophistication and inventiveness. No doubt they will unfold further on drawing boards and computer screens this winter. How I look forward to meeting the intelligences which can continue to dream up designs of this quality.

The season also seemed to end sooner and without a 'Grand Finale'. It may be that Brian Grist was completely correct in his article The Aquifer Attractor and perhaps the water table, in this hottest of summers, became too low for the microwaves, or whatever, to operate efficiently. As reported by a Dutch couple at The Barge Inn, Holland had 26 formations last year, but this year only four by mid-July.

Another shock this year was the total absence of formations in the beloved East Field of Alton Barnes, site of the 1990 Led Zeppelin album cover. How many of us, in our wildest dreams, would have anticipated this after such a consistent recurrence since. The farmer, Tim Carson, admitted he was pleased to be passed over while Polly, his wife, seemed to be disappointed. Perhaps this is another lesson for us. Have no expectations.

* * * * *

The king of croppie pubs, The Barge Inn in Honey Street, had a brilliant season. We are lucky to have found such an idyllic headquarters with such tolerant and flexible hosts. There was an evening in mid-August when, apart from the usual suspects, we had an American group, a German group, led by Michael Hesemann and an American TV news team. One could barely squeeze in.

* * * * *

The circle phenomenon is the most photogenic we have ever seen and everyone wants a ride on the bus. At the Whole Life Expo, a kind of American New Age Marks and Spencer in Pasadena last May, there were four or five speakers whose programme notes promised exciting images and information about the circles. Everyone is onto it. Crop Circles and past Life Regression. The Native American Way of Crop Circles, Crop Circle Cuisine for Vegetarians, How to Make Friends and Influence People with Crop Circles.

My new video *The Kennedy Assassination and the Crop Circles* will be a real hit.

* * * * *

The Centre for Crop Circles Studies really seems to have sunk to the lowest level of awfulness. Accusations and counterclaims. Letters and resignations. Worst of all, hatreds and terrible insults.

How has it come to this? Most of us, though there are exceptions, believe that we are dealing with a spiritual phenomenon. Many of us feel that the crop circles are teachers. How have they allowed us – how could we allow ourselves? – to sink so low?

We must remember the privilege of our involvement with the circles. Like all privileges, it carries obligations.

I could not help thinking, during the last horrible weeks, that this – in a perverse kind of way – is the ultimate victory for the Dougs and Daves, for the debunkers and hoaxers, for the whole unpleasant crew. And, imagine the nightmare if the tabloids got hold of it. 'Crop Circle Cranks Squabble', 'Crop Circle Club Splits', CCCS. I offer a prize for the best tabloid-style screamer.

* * * * *

In 1994, the most difficult part of the work on the seasonal *Crop Circle Calendar* was the selection of images from the riches of that season. My artistic director and I did our best but, predictably, when our list was presented, certain members of Council were most concerned. They felt, as usual without a shred of evidence, that some of the chosen circles were suspect. We were required to print a silly disclaimer on the cover. (Disclaiming what? Our contention that all circles are caused by the spirits of dead turkeys?)

This year's calendar is, sadly, a terrible disappointment. With thirteen full-colour pages, it shows no more than six formations from this brilliant season. The omissions are shocking and, once again, I find myself asking if someone knows something that the rest of us don't.

And then it was whispered to me that several of the six included were ones that were ADAS-approved. Ah. That's alright then.

ADAS, you will remember, were the people who let us know, to howls of derision from the Exmoor farming community, that there really was no beast there! What had been seen was a large domestic cat. The photos, films and videos were, likewise, a very big kitty. The savage mutilations of farm animals were the work of scavengers, after death had occurred by natural causes. Once again, it's business as usual. We are not to worry our little heads.

Unlike Dr. Mike Foley of ADAS who, shortly before he was fired, discovered that there was a tangible change in soils inside crop formations. Scratching his head he is reported to have said "Hoaxers might be thinking two steps ahead of us and are doing something to create a biological difference inside and outside the formation" *Western Daily Press*, 24/9/95.

* * * * *

It helps to remember that science has become the most powerful religious orthodoxy on the planet. Like all religions, it serves to comfort us in the face of the fearfully unknown and inexplicable. Its main weapons are exclusion and denial. It solidifies and consolidates the existing acceptable world view and scoffs at all challenges.

Those most aware of and damaged by this denial are those scientists who have themselves dared to venture a slightly unorthodox idea. Can anyone imagine a mechanism more impossible to breach, more efficiently committed to the prevention of imagination and change, than 'peer review'?

We might have our knowledge and understanding increased by the work of committed, individual scientists working alone, but to expect a scientific institution to grant us the comfort of their seal of approval is folly.

1996

The circles draw me once again to America where I am doing a few lectures on the 1995 season. I have spent several days hunched over a light-box, selecting and arranging slides. What I find astonishing is that, after all these talks, these beautiful images remain enchanting and mystifying. The people who will see these photographs will be delighted. To a greater or lesser extent, they will be changed.

I remain convinced that we are in the present of magic.

* * * * *

As Robert Downey Jr. says in *Air America*, "No need to give up a good theory just because it isn't true".

The recent Carl Sagan article is very significant. Why does a figure of Sagan's importance take time to rubbish the crop circles? He knows that they are man-made though he can cite no evidence. He talks approvingly of the "athletic" Doug and Dave, the "artists" who he has not met, but nevertheless believes. He talks arrogantly about "shoddy.... standards of evidence" but all the evidence he cites himself is third-hand and anecdotal. Nothing in his grubby little piece is new.

Those elements which are more difficult to understand or debunk are blithely ignored. How does he deal with the matter of many designs appearing over a single, short summer's night? He averts his gaze. How does he deal with the question of the manifestation of circles in the middle of huge North American fields without farmers' tramlines for access? Well, he simply doesn't. What does he say about the multiple sightings of strange lights and luminosities around the circles? Totally disregarded!

Instead he trots out the stale old routines and attempts to do what he set out to do and what he is famous for – debunking.

OK, America, you can go back to sleep now. One would like to say that if this is the best science can do at the end of our century, then God help us. It's not worth saying because, tragically, he is the best science can do. But his most significant phrase is "… how belief systems widely held and supported by the political, religious and academic hierarchies often turn out to be not just slightly in error but grotesquely wrong". Well, exactly, Carl!

* * * * *

When positions are about to shift cataclysmically, the defence of the status quo becomes most vehement. Just prior to revolutions, the establishment is most ruthless. Change is always heralded by a desperation, on the part of the authorities, to maintain convention.

I had been deeply irritated by the sequence of self-righteous debunkers but, over the last weeks, I have come to see how reassuring they are. The Sagans and their cohorts evince nothing more than the anxiety of a hollow and discredited ideology. I don't know for sure what is behind the circles, but I am sure of two things; Doug and Dave have nothing to do with it and the likes of Sagan, with their patronising denials and certainties, are laughable.

It must be awful to scoff, constantly, at the ideas of others. The only thing we can be certain of is that change is constant. Change is the water we swim in. The pages of history are littered with sad and sanctimonious souls who, despite overwhelming evidence, assert that today's consensus must be an eternal truth. They are reinforced by the fact that society always regards new ideas with suspicion. Scoffers have the cowards' advantage: cheap shots at soft targets.

* * * * *

As science thus coagulates to a grotesque travesty, it is a delight to find individual scientists who have the courage, curiosity and imagination to put their heads above the trenches and explore the unconventional. Dr. Levengood, of the Pinelandia Biophysical lab in Michigan, is one and another is our own Jim Lyons.

Levengood's work on the changes in plants involved in crop circles compared to plants outside the formations is clear proof of a high energy event taking place, similar to a microwave, and not replicable by hoaxers.

Jim's talk at the London Winter Lecture Series was a dazzling and provocative event. The range of his knowledge and the strength of his enthusiasm are infectious. He is working tentatively towards a theory of unified energies; a theory which must include, he believes, Neolithic sites and human consciousness.

Jim Lyons is worth a thousand Sagans.

* * * * *

I had a call this afternoon from the BBC. They have some programme which confronts perpetrators with their victims. They are planning to confront a hoax claimant with his victim farmer. The former, contrite, will confess and seek absolution; the latter, though aggrieved, will forgive. It sounds like a million laughs – a sort of croppie Oprah.

The problem, the young researcher explained, was that, amusing though the programme would be, very few people knew about crop circles. Would I be the "expert" to explain the subject prior to the confrontation? I told him that there could be no experts in the unknown and that, in any case, I could not be on a programme which trivialised a subject dear to my heart.

* * * * *

I recently offered a prize for the best tabloid style screamer based on the initials CCCS. In the opinion of the judges, the best four entries, of no lest than twelve submission, were: Croppie Cranks Commit Suicide – Corn Circle Centre Sinks – Corny Croppies' Crisis Showdown – Crisis Causes Croppies' Strife. Sadly, I must admit that all twelve entries were from the only competitor, Graham Holman of Sussex. The prize is on its way!

* * * * *

Some time ago I was invited to lecture on the circles at the Architectural Association, the school where I studied more years ago than I care to admit. I must say, however, that they were delighted and, when the talk was finished, I was surrounded by students who were aggrieved by the fact that they had known absolutely nothing about these wonders.

It has been clear for years that we are dealing here with two astonishments. First, the crop circle phenomenon itself and, second, that the roads to Wiltshire and Hampshire are not black with sightseers' cars every summer. How could it be that year after year, just two hours from London, we receive miracles which are, in the public realm, totally ignored?

I try not to be a conspiracy theorist. I avoid paranoia. However, there can no longer be any doubt that since the Doug and Dave nonsense, the management of crop circle misinformation has been amazingly successful. Who has orchestrated it and on whose behalf? They are a) very skillful and b) very frightened.

* * * * *

During questions, a nice girl asked, "How do you get these beautiful photos? Does the Royal Air Force send them to you?"

What a wonderful vision.

"Hello. RAF Brize Norton, Strategic Bomber Command. Can I help you?"

"Yes, Michael Green here, Chairman of the CCCS. Could I speak to Air Marshall Simpson?"

"Hello Michael. Buffy Simpson here. I suppose you're calling about that astonishing formation at Avebury."

"Yes, That's right, Buffy."

"Well, don't worry. I've only just seen the photos myself. What

45

a beauty! I'll put them on a bike to you right away. Sorry for the delay."

Meanwhile, in a bunker deep below the Rocky Mountains a satellite technician calls his supervisor at the pentagon.

"Good morning Sir. Today's first sweep across southern England has shown a fantastic circle at Alton Barnes. I have dispatched a copy to the CCCS in England and also to the Dreads. I guess you would like to look at it yourself."

Helicopter squadrons, as usual, are ferrying old ladies into town to do their shopping. The Royal Navy is running boat trips for holidaymakers and seamanship weekends for the young. The army continues its programmes of city cleaning and park maintenance. The cavalry is giving free riding lessons and the Medical Corps, as usual, is assisting at the hospitals.

* * * * *

The Winter Lecture series continues its illuminating progress. The February speaker dealt with recent years' attempts, by a group of Sussex croppies and with the help of a psychic, to establish tangible and meaningful contact with the circle makers. The video of the medium making contact, on site, with an intelligence which identified itself as from Sirius was, it was generally agreed, powerfully emotional.

* * * * *

A few weekends ago I went to Glastonbury and, on the way down, I couldn't resist the urge to pass through Alton Barnes. A few years ago I hadn't even heard of the place and now it has a curious hold on my affections. I guess I'm not alone. Though there was snow around, East Field was entirely green. What could that be? Was it early crop or simply the Earth insisting that soil should be greened over?

It was the afternoon and The Barge Inn was closed. The canal was frozen over. We are truly blessed with that place. Not only are the landlord and lady hospitable and tolerant beyond belief but it must be one of the most beautifully located pubs in Britain.

It is clear that the centre of activity has moved southward from Wiltshire towards Hampshire. East Field was untouched last year. There is a shift, almost a precession of energies. I think the centre will shift through Hampshire towards Surrey and Sussex.

As usual, I have absolutely no evidence on which to base this arrogant prediction.

* * * * *

Live TV, a company I had not heard of, asked me to appear on a late night interview show. I was led to believe that the half-hour programme would be devoted to an interview on the circles.

Prior to the interview, I was put in a corner outside the studio with a TV to watch. When I saw that the programme before mine was *Topless Darts* I realised that it would be downhill all the way. Let me explain *Topless Darts*. Two young women, dressed only in bikini bottoms – I swear! – play darts on a sunny beach. The winner gets a T-shirt.

But the real horror was yet to come. Instead of an interview, this was a ragbag of a programme called *Weird Night*, with crystal-ball gazers, a tarot reader in funny clothes and, as you would expect, assorted weirdos. There was a live link-up with New York where it was explained how we could hear our "departed loved ones" by staring at a blank TV screen at 3.00am and listening to the hiss. I had three minutes to deal with the most superficial questions. "So tell us all, Michael, who's doing it then? Is it those little green men?" asked the blonde interviewer in the sparkly black top.

Your deeply embarrassed weirdo columnist has had to endure merciless torment from friends ever since.

This afternoon, as I was writing the above, I heard news of the season's first formations, in Kent and Cambridgeshire. Another brilliant summer ahead. As I said last year, here we go again!

* * * * *

I am spending the summer in Wiltshire, ten minutes from the East Field formation and half an hour from the Stonehenge beauty. The Alton Barnes white horse is visible from my bedroom window.

By several fortunate coincidences, Patricia and I were in the first group to go into the Stonehenge circle. Like the East Field DNA helix it is beautiful and enormous. It measures 915′ 6″ along the spine. Also like East Field its complex shape is formed of nothing but circles, 151 here, of varied size.

It was too big to read clearly from the ground; aerial images were needed to clarify it. But on the spot its circles demonstrated a range of swirl and lay which seemed like an encyclopaedia of circle-making skills. The centres of the smaller circles were a particular astonishment for their stylistic diversity. As you walked from one another they seemed to say "look what else we can do!".

* * * * *

The Stonehenge formation has produced three remarkable stories. Like all tales in this business they are anecdotal. They shift, Chinese Whisper-like, in every retelling. However they seem to check out.

First. An air-taxi pilot flew in to Thruxton, passing over the field at 5.30pm in the afternoon. There was no formation. He came back by the field within the hour and the circles had arrived. This account is supported by a gamekeeper who apparently saw a clear field during the afternoon and a Stonehenge guard who noticed the circle in the early evening. Thus we seem to have confirmation of a daylight appearance though – of course – nobody has yet claimed to have observed it.

Second. The farmer was incandescent with rage at the "vandals" who had damaged his crop. He refused under any circumstances to allow access and actually turned away when he was shown the photograph. Several people (all women, of course) tried to reason with him, explaining that because of its scale and beauty and also because of its prominent location, it would be impossible to keep people away. Why could he not charge for access and make money? He was intractable and threatened to bring in the machines to cut it out, but that evening, without warning, a huge sign went up by the road saying "Come and see Europe's best crop circle!" His son was posted by the gate and there was an unending stream of visitors. Everyone was happy.

Third. In the middle of these discussions the farmer said he had confirmation that it was man-made. There had been a call, anonymous needless to say, from a young man who claimed to have made it. He was most apologetic and offered the farmer £500 in compensation.

This signalled to me at least, an escalation in the sophistication of the Circle Claimants' tactics. There was a moment when it appeared the hoax supporters might be upping the stakes. However, the farmer eventually admitted he had made up the story to discourage interest!

* * * * *

Sitting in one of the lovely Chiselden formations, Patricia says "Oh (expletive deleted). A coach tour."

A tenacious crocodile of determined middle-aged American women (why are they always women?) stomps along the tram line towards us. We scoop up our stuff and make for the other tram line. Too late. They're in. As we scurry away a voice calls: "Michael, Michael, I have a question for you."

I vaguely recognise a face from the Glastonbury Symposium and, as I now realise, having spoken there, I am "Michael", public property.

"You know the Stonehedge formation..."

"Stonehenge" I murmur.

". . yes, the Juliette set..."

"Well, some people have decided to call it the Julia set..." I say.

"...yes, well, Colon Andrews..."

"It's pronounced 'Colin' here." I say. "Colon is a part of the lower digestive tract."

".... yes, well, I bought this photo of the Stonehedge Juliette set from Colon Andrews and it's been stolen from my hotel room."

My mind goes into melt-down. What can this little woman want? Why did she make me stop my rapid escape down the tramline? Does she think I am an insurance agent, a private detective? Does she think I looted her hotel room?

I glance longingly at Patrica's distant back. She's made it.

"I am sure Mr. Andrews will happily sell you another photograph." I say reassuringly.

"Yes. But where is he? Where is he?"

I, in turn, flee.

* * * * *

Early on the evening of 11th August we had word that a large formation had arrived at Oliver's Castle. I raced there with Patricia and a German video maker and we arrived at the edge as the dusk, and a savage rainstorm, moved in.

Oliver's Castle is the best location for looking down on crop circles. Below us as the light dimmed and the rain pelted we saw the lovely Snowflake formation. It was delightful. We staggered back through the mud. Three pairs of shoes ruined.

The farmer at Roundway Farm is one of the most difficult I have every met. When I approached him for permission to go in and measure, he rudely refused and said the formation was the result of "vandalism". Some days later we were shocked to see that he had deliberately driven his combine harvester through the heart of the Snowflake, leaving the rest of the field intact, although viewed from the hill above it was clear that enough remained for us to measure. We found him again, valiantly resisted our urge to discuss vandalism with him, offered him cash, and with his purchased permission, drove to the field.

A short digression here about town planning. The Grand Boulevards of Paris are considered masterpieces of urbanism. What is little known is that Paris had been the densest and most squalid of cities. It was disease-ridden and suffered regular revolutions. The boulevards were ruthlessly driven through the city by Baron Hausmann, not to make the beauty that Paris now is, but to provide rapid access for the army to quell revolution wherever it might occur. The clearing of terrible slums was an accidental advantage. Digression ends.

We arrived at the edge of the field to find a truly Hausmannian boulevard welcoming us. It stretched, straight and wide, across the field. There was no alternative – really there wasn't – but to drive ceremonially to the centre of the circle. I am proud to claim to be the first person ever to drive into a circle (or more correctly, for the more squeamish readers, into the former, now destroyed, site of a circle.)

When we had finished measuring, we turned the car by driving around the largely wrecked central circle. With the flow of course. With the flow.

54

1997

One morning, we drove by the East Field at Alton Barnes to see the pattern of the harvested Double Helix formation beautifully duplicated in bright green shoots in the stubble. The Barley seeds which had been pressed into the earth by so many visitors had started to grow. We took photographs and went for lunch. On our return it had been ploughed in. The cycle continues. We have not the remotest idea what the soil of East Field will offer us next season.

* * * * *

I think it would be churlish to allow the rumoured recent death of Dave Chorley (of Doug and Dave fame, for younger readers) to pass unremarked. Dave was the smaller and less unpleasant of the two. I never met him but he unfortunately became – for me as for many of us – a familiar part of the landscape. How many questions after lectures have been dominated by the media sculpted view of D & D and how truly nasty were the results of their deceptions. We rarely get questions about Doug and Dave anymore. They are a minor grubby footnote in the history of a breathtaking world phenomenon but, in a curious way, I am sorry to see him go. He was the milder and less vehement of the two and I always had the impression that Dave, unlike Doug who still clings to his legend like a condemned man to his alibi, found the whole episode distasteful.

We missed an opportunity. When he and Doug quarrelled over money, Dave, isolated and lonely, was often seen around the pubs of Portsmouth. I am sure, given the right kind of nudge, beans would have been spilled.

* * * * *

More on the scuzzier side. (Why does it always seem to fall to me to deal with the scuzzy?) I read in a local paper some weeks ago that there was to be an art show dealing with ETs, UFOs and crop circles. One "Rod Dickinson, the World's Leading Crop Circle Artist" was to attend. I did not go, but a friend who did tells me that "Rod Dickinson" was there using the 1997 calendar which I helped to design as his principal piece of evidence.

Some time later, he was interviewed by Michael Lindemann who is a UFO commentator in the US and – transformed now into "Rodney Dickinson" – he persuaded his host that he knew who had made the huge 1996 Stonehenge formation. Needless to say, Lindemann, as always in these situations, was blissfully ignorant of the facts surrounding the Stonehenge events, and swallowed the story whole.

So there we have it. Stonehenge is man-made, Dickinson said so, Lindemann believed him, and, reportedly, a "leading researcher" was "on the verge" of declaring it a hoax. All we need now is for a "leading crop circle magazine" to feature this undiscerning and unappetising chain of untruth and the cycle will be completed.

Dickinson is a liar who has to travel 8000 miles to find a credulous audience. Lindemann is rather irresponsible and should know better than to lend his name to this kind of garbage. And the others? Well, I think they know....

* * * * *

On a less distasteful note, I will be doing a talk on the circles for a US operation called The Learning Annex who run continuous courses on a variety of subjects. It is – I suppose – a kind of New Age, self-improvement, adult education emporium. The range of offerings might be amusing.

First, personal relationships. How To Marry Rich reminds us that The Rich Are Going To Marry…Why Not To You?…You can attend 10 Fatal Dating Mistakes (And How to Avoid Them!) or What Women Really Want in Bed. You can learn how to Create A Native American prayer Arrow, Start A Gift-Basket Business, or Make Your Own Soaps. For your health, you can learn The Art of Breathing, Non-Surgical Facelifts, or How To Cook Two Weeks of Healthy Inexpensive Meals (In One Evening!) More remarkably you could study Transformational Haircutting which will show you how to style your hair to complement your aura.

The brochure is almost 50 pages long and these samples are taken from just the first 15 pages. The most important point (which I make with some shame) is the fact that course 211A, Crop Circles & Sacred Geometry is the cheapest course available. Not in the cheaper group, the cheapest! What are they trying to tell me?

* * * * *

At last it has arrived! Someone has filmed what appears to be the formation of a crop circle. A young man called John Weyleigh spent the night (a very wet night) on top of Oliver's Castle on a crop-watch. He was awoken by strange noises and looked down into the field to see strange lights. He grabbed his camera and recorded two pairs of lights moving deliberately above the field in a smooth arc. Only when he viewed the tape through his TV did he notice that a crop circle had formed below the luminosities.

There was a showing of the tape at The Barge. The overwhelming sense it generated, for me at least, was the smoothness and control of the operation.

A good circle is always breathtaking because it seems so easy. The crop appears to have been laid down with the confidence that only comes with absolute proficiency. It is impossible to experience without admiration for the authors. A beautiful circle embodies both the strength and accuracy of a tennis champion's forehand and the grace and immediacy of a Japanese master's brushstroke on rice paper. Somehow the Oliver's Castle video touches the heart in exactly the same way and this is why I am certain of its authenticity.

* * * * *

As soon as a number of whizzkid croppies were shown the Oliver's Castle video they declared, publicly and with confidence, that they would be able to duplicate it without much trouble.

Those who saw their copies were stunned by the professionalism and veracity. So successful were they that immediate offers came from Spielberg's Dreamworks asking them to head their electronic special effects division. The deal was about to be signed when George Lucas flew in with his private jet bearing a hugely superior counter-offer. These whizzkids, we understand, blew Steven out, accepted the Lucas deal and will be taking up their positions as Vice Presidents of Special Effects at Industrial Light and Magic in northern California within the next few days.

What is amazing, after these people's scoops, is the astonishing number of high-level video and computer professionals and academics who have been completely taken in and have testified to the veracity of the original Weyleigh footage. Poor saps!

* * * * *

I get a few letters, some approving and some not, but, in the last month, I received a letter which verged on hate-mail. Of course, I would never dignify this junk with a reply, but I get an enormous amount of pleasure from the fact that this guy cannot spell, punctuate or make coherent sentences. Above all, he does not possess the tiniest vestige of humour.

To help such people, I must state that the previous section of writing here is not true. It is ironic. I-R-O-N-I-C. Look it up.

* * * * *

The scene is an outer chamber of Limbo, reserved for those of deeply blotched Karma waiting to hear where they are to be sent in penance. A serious looking intellectual sits pensively on a cloud, chin on hand in the position of Rodin's Thinker.

Carl Sagan (for it is he): "How could I have been so stupid? I knew those CSICOP guys were flaky as soon as I set eyes on them. And then that cheesy 'Amazing Randi'! My promising career in Science ruined to end up doing PR with a vaudeville conjurer."

A short figure in a grubby raincoat with a back-to-front baseball cap shuffles into view. He stops in surprise at the sight of Sagan and he approaches nervously.

Dave Chorley (for it is he): "Excuse me, sir, but weren't you Carl Sagan?"

Sagan (animated): "Jimmy! Jim Schnabel! Is it you?"

Chorley sheepishly rotates his cap to reveal a bent paper clip on the brim.

Chorley: "I'm very honoured to meet you, sir, and I'd like to take this opportunity to thank you for that nice chapter in your latest, er, last book."

Sagan: "And who were you?"

Chorley: "I was Dave of the famous Doug and Dave team who made all the crop circles as you noted in your excellent book, sir."

Sagan: "You've not been here very long have you?"

Chorley: "No, sir. Just arrived, as it happens."

Sagan: "Well, when you've been here another aeon or two you'll understand how things work up here. No lies allowed. No exaggerations, distortions or economies with the truth. No fibs, falsehoods or deceptions. We all have access to truth here. I am afraid we can all see right through each other. I now know what I have to admit I suspected all along. You were a couple of old frauds."

Chorley (chastened): "Ok, you're right. It wasn't my idea. I just went along for the ride. It was Doug who..."

Sagan: "But you liked the cash..."

Chorley: "And seeing as we're being truthful, so did you! And I have to tell you that the chapter on crop circles was pure garbage. We laughed 'til we wept."

Sagan (sighing): "I know, I know. There is a certain irony in our being called here at about the same time. I wonder what it means?"

Chorley (nervously, after a moment's silence): "What happens next?"

Sagan: "Oh, they'll call you in to assess your case and then you're sent out here for a century or two to await their decision."

Chorley finds a cloud to sit on. Darkness falls.

(Later) IT IS THE DECISION OF THIS COURT:

Sagan C. will spend the next incarnation as Chairman of the Centre for Crop Circle Studies.

Chorley D. will spend the next three incarnations as Editor of *The Sussex Circular*.

* * * * *

Oh dear. Once again I am accused by no less than TWO of the dotty old first-generation 'researchers' of stating that "there are no hoaxes". While I usually prefer to charitably leave their delusional mumblings unchecked, I must set the record straight.

Of course there have been, there are and undoubtedly there will be hoaxes. My argument is that they are so few that the hoax component of the crop circle phenomenon is of no significance. Apart, that is, from the insight it offers to certain people's paranoia.

These two old frauds are currently asserting that 70% and 90% of the UK's 1996 formations were hoaxes. By my calculation this is, respectively, two hundred and twelve and two hundred and seventy-three formations.

These are very interesting claims and any information in support of such surrealism must be welcomed by every researcher. However, both Mr. 70% and Mr. 90% have doggedly resisted any attempt to draw them out further than their regularly repeated statements.

I have long argued that the high (and always rounded-off) percentage figure is given by a scoundrel to support the insupportable. Why is it never 68% or 83%? I'll tell you why. Because it is never based on evidence but always on an emotional feeling. For 70% or 90% read "Many. A lot. Countless. Numerous. Abundant. Plentiful. And anyway, a big percentage figure will testify to my significance. "

Now, everyone is entitled to their opinion. Does it need to be restated that people may believe whatever they want? However, when their view is trumpeted so widely, so loudly and with such Mussolini-esque authority as fact, I think we have the right to call them to account.

So here is a challenge. It would change the nature of crop circle studies if these numbers were supported. We would all benefit and thank our distinguished friends. And so I dare them to demonstrate, not repeat claims or opinions, but prove hoaxes. Fifty would be too onerous, so let's stick with twenty. Well, even twenty is hard. No, I don't think they could handle that. How about ten?

That's it! I challenge them to demonstrate, to prove beyond doubt, that ten formations were hoaxed in 1996.

I breathlessly await their responses.

* * * * *

A company somewhere in Texas is offering novel funeral arrangements. For $4,600 they will put your ashes (clearly you have to be cremated first) into orbit. The news this evening showed a film of the first launch.

Something looking scarily like a Cruise Missile blasts skyward carrying, we are told, the remains of both Dr. Timothy Leary and Gene Roddenberry. My respect for you, dear reader, is such that I know I need not explain their importance in our lifetimes or the frisson delivered by their conjunction here. They were accompanied, the voice-over tells us, by twenty-two others, each neatly contained in a small aluminium canister.

Now let's see. $4,600 times twenty-four is...

* * * * *

The Oliver's Castle video touched me deeply. It seemed to be right. A truly impressive array of film, video and special effects people were most impressed. Not a single one said that it could not be faked. They all agreed that it could. But it would take time, money, equipment and real skill and artistry. Attempts by amateurs to duplicate it were laughable.

The obsession on the part of the principal hoax-boosters to discredit the video at any cost became almost comic. The target of their attack was the hapless Weyleigh or Wabe. He worked in a video company, he had dyed his hair, he had grown – or was it shaved off? – a beard, since first appearing. The first thing he told us was that he wanted nothing except to be left alone but they invaded his place of work, unannounced and mob-handed, with a Japanese film crew. They reported, like schoolboy paparazzi, that he ran away. Wouldn't you run away?

I knew that formation and I know it to be real. Measuring it, we noted several exquisite features of construction. There was nothing there to raise our suspicions. When the formation was put on the drawing board, it unfolded like a flower, revealing many particular characteristics. Perhaps the most important of these was that it contained – though clearly a six-fold figure – a thin seven-fold star, a heptagram. This is a significant discovery as not only is this the first time seven-fold geometry has been found but this is the geometry of Spirit and Revelation. What could be a more appropriate additional gift?

* * * * *

I have never met Tony Nash and I don't know who he is but I am so grateful for his recent letter. A breath of fresh air. Indeed air so fresh that I assume he is – even now – considering several offers from journals and organisations.

Thank you, Tony Nash.

* * * * *

Once again the season has started at a breathtaking level. Last year, with the arrival of the Alton Barnes 'DNA' formation on the 17th June, a new record was established for the earliness of such a complex design. Who would have believed that, this year, a major crop circle would arrive in mid-April? They are clearly trying to get our attention. As with last year, if only we could look and listen, we could understand that clear messages are being sent. The sophisticated Stonehenge snowflake, a formation of true finesse, cannot be read as anything but a strong confirmation of the Oliver's Castle events last year. No doubt some fool will emerge to characterise even this as a hoax.

* * * * *

As the season opens, it is appropriate, especially for newer recruits, to quote a couple of rules from *Cornography's Guidance for the Perplexed Croppie* which is now available in all good bookshops.

RULE 161. "THE WEB IS FULL OF GARBAGE". Like all the rules in this excellent little book, they are occasionally wrong (i.e. the exception of Crop Circle Connector). But only occasionally. It is safe to assume with the internet that the photographs are good, the diagrams are inaccurate and the opinions veer from blah to outright lunacy. Read them if (a) you have no interest in the crop circles or (b) you have no life.

RULE 247. "ANYONE TELLING YOU A CIRCLE IS HOAXED IS A LIAR". 247 is broken, on average, only once or twice a year. Generally it is as good as gold. Experience has shown that the likelihood of hoax information being invented through wild opinion, distortion, fear or some other kind of psychopathology is now so overwhelming that RULE 247 has taken its place as the most useful of all. If when you are told a circle is hoaxed you immediately respond "Liar!" the party will usually slink away. He (for it is always he) normally has an awe-struck audience for his fantasies. Respond with vigour or ask questions. You will be helping us all.

A combination of 161 and 247 proves particularly useful.

* * * * *

The closest field to where Patricia Murray and I stay in Wiltshire is Gypsy patch in Etchilhampton. This is the field that received the eight tenths of a mile long formation last year. In the way of croppies everywhere, we took it as a personal gift because it landed the day we spoke at Glastonbury. Another speaker who spoke the same day and who was staying with us a mile from the field felt that the formation was of real significance for him, too.

Patricia and I assumed we would get another this year in our neighbouring field and, on the 24th July, in the dark, a large luminosity whizzed past us towards the field. We took this as an omen and visited the field daily. On the night of Wednesday 30th July, driving home from Devizes, I turned the corner near the field and blurted out "It's landed!". I have never done this kind of thing before and I was as surprised to hear it as Patricia. She said, trying to humour me, I thought – "What's it like?". I replied "It's three circles" with a similar certainty. To this day I have no idea how I got this information. The following afternoon, we went to the field and discovered the twin formations; a six-fold spinning star and the 'Calendar Grid', the first large square ever.

Compare, for a moment, our delight at this discovery (a delight which is there for anybody who wishes to be involved with the circles) to the sleazy satisfactions derived by the know-it-all debunkers, whose greatest thrill is to diminish wonder and steal joy.

The fact that there were only two circles did not bother me a great deal. After all, I had no idea where the information came from. I was hardly in a position to moan about its inaccuracy!

The Calendar Grid was a huge 100′ square set within a 150′ circle. The square was divided into 780 smaller squares, 30 east-west and 26 north-south, by laid grid-lines, about eleven or twelve inches wide. The grid systems both commenced at the north-west corner of the square, horizontal lines laid first and then vertical. They were laid boustrophedon, which means 'as the ox ploughs', that is left to right then right to left or up, down, up, down. Thus the lines followed a continuous snake-like path of well over two and a half thousand feet in length.

We called it a Calendar Grid because we felt that the 26 units represented 26 weeks, or half a year. 30 lines of 26 thus was fifteen years which brought us to – wait for it – 2012, the date signalled so clearly by the Mayan calendar.

Do I need to describe the joy of this work? Do I need to clarify my sadness at the thought of those pub-rats whose idea of research is to sit with a beer and proclaim their groundless doubts to anyone stupid enough to give them time?

* * * * *

Yesterday we spent three hours in the field watching the formations being harvested. Watching a harvester cut a formation away is always moving, especially if it has been important to you and if you have spent time there. As the machine moved up and down, I lay in the formations and examined my surroundings in the minutest detail. It had never occurred to me that there were so many wild flowers in a wheat field, possibly because they are so tiny. I had never been so clearly aware of the number of insects that live in this environment. Nor had I spent so long staring, really staring, at one square foot of laid crop circle. There is so much to learn.

As the harvester sliced into the formations it revealed, as it always does, the shadow of the circle. The laid crop is generally below the blades and the pattern is sometimes clearer after harvest. In the case of the grid, it was exposed as an even more astonishing creation.

To our amazement, the combine harvester stopped. The driver wanted to speak to us. This is unheard of as they are under great pressure to get the harvest in and to move on to the next farm. He leaned out of the cab and said "Have you seen the third circle?" Apparently, some distance away, there was a simple circle. My informants had been correct!

* * * * *

Returning to California after this most surprising of seasons, leaves me, still in October, completely zapped. A re-entry to the real world after three months of the surreal. But who would claim that California is the real world?

I spent the autumn (or 'fall' as I must learn to say) producing accurate scale drawings of formations. This is a contemplative – even meditative – ritual which brings me so much real satisfaction that its anticipation softens the blow of the end of the season. It becomes an extension of the season for me as I have to spend days close to the detail, dimension, proportion and geometry of each formation. The wall behind the drawing board is covered with photographs. No matter how accurate the measurements, the spirit and character of the shape has to be incorporated. This is difficult to explain.

In the early hours of last night I finished my drawing of the Milk Hill formation. There has been much talk of its 198 circles. Personally, I never bothered to count. All I know is that when you spend hour after hour positioning, sizing, drawing, and filling in these circles, you enter a truly focused state in which a closeness to the form (and even, dare I suggest, to the intelligence which originated it) becomes inevitable.

I have no doubt that everybody interested in circles should draw from their photographs, no matter how crudely. There is so much for everybody to learn from this exercise. In many ways, the confrontation with the circles' essence which results from hours working on a drawing is more direct than that which most people can achieve in the formation itself.

It should never be done quickly. Too much can be missed.

* * * * *

Some of you may have heard my intemperate little outburst at the Glastonbury Conference this summer where I vented my anger at the hoax boosters who masquerade as researchers and poison the well for everybody. I hoped that this would be some kind of catharsis which would allow me to stay clear and get on with my work.

But it doesn't go away. Perhaps I am having to redeem myself for sins committed in previous lifetimes. One critic has implied that I advocate book-burnings and censorship. Before I get my jackboots fitted I must try to conclude this matter once and for all. Crop circles are a mystery. Nobody can explain them. For many, the inexplicable is intolerable so they cling to the old discredited hoax hypothesis. There was a time when this might have been believable but, in 1997, it can only be sustained by blind faith. Why is there never (not rarely, but never) any evidence?

How can these people continue to address the miraculous as vandalism, high art as petty crime? When someone provides hard evidence for hoaxes (or even one hoax) we might discuss it. Until then don't hold your breath.

* * * * *

A whole thesis could be devoted to the quintuplet. This form was for me the first incontrovertible evidence of the intelligence behind the circles. They always seemed to obey four design rules in their construction. First, they conformed top right angle geometry. Second, the centre circle was always larger than the four satellites. Third, the four satellites were of equal diameter and, fourth, the satellites were the same distance from their mother circle. These rules were rarely broken.

At a lecture in 1995 the audience suggested that they meditate on a shape for the forthcoming season. I had spoken about quintuplet geometry and – rather unimaginatively I thought – they wished for a quintuplet. (I should mention here that an audience this spring chose a hexagon. We were doubtful and said that, although six-fold geometry had been common for years, the hexagon was unknown. I need not point out just how successful they were.) The Santa Barbara people were rewarded with the 1995 'quintuplet of quintuplets' at Telegraph Hill, a form never before or since recorded. Looking back, with the experience of the beautiful Koch snowflakes this year, a quintuplet of quintuplets is also a kind of fractal. Just as the triangles of the

Koch fractals could, theoretically, reduce and reproduce infinitely, so could the quintuplet satellites themselves become smaller quintuplets ad infinitum. With the snow flakes the process stopped at the third iteration when the technology of wheat bending reached its limits. This was the point at which triangles were replaced by circles.

And this season, the sharp-eyed will have noticed two new games being played within the quintuplet rules.

1998

Part of the protocol of living around LA is that you leave the stars alone, for they are everywhere. For Patricia, who has lived here most of her life, this is almost second nature while I, a naïve English film buff, tend to behave disgracefully.

The other day Nicolas Cage, with two others, sat at a table on the pavement (or sidewalk as I must learn to say) of a little Italian restaurant we were visiting. This was more than I could bear! I had our Crop Circle Calendar with me and I went outside to give him a copy. I have to say he was astonished by the photographs. One of his companions was Jim Carrey who made the kind of comments with which by now we are all familiar. But Cage was impressed and, after looking through the images, handed it across the table to the third member of the party, who looked incongruously like an over weight middle-aged biker. As soon as he got it, the waiter arrived with their food. The biker put the calendar on his substantial thighs and began to eat. I could not see what was going on but Patricia, who was in a better position, reported to me. Olive oil and pizza rained down on the cover. He was using it as a napkin to protect his trousers.

They ate quickly and the biker came in to pay. Cage, it was reported to me, picked up the calendar and tenderly wiped the food off the cover. That is more like it, I thought. The Oscar winner shows appropriate respect for the miraculous.

The biker, having paid, went out. They all left. The waiter came in with the calendar and told us that it had been left behind.

What, if any, is the moral of this story?

A) Nicolas Cage, confronting the horror of his thoughtless action, recognises the importance of these images which he so thoughtlessly abandoned. He cannot sleep, he cannot work, he drinks and becomes a shadow of his former self. Hollywood abandons him. He is history.

B) Nicolas Cage, confronting the horror of his thoughtless action, recognises the importance of these images which he so thoughtlessly abandoned. He haunts the restaurant hoping to meet us again. He hires the best detective agencies to make contact with us. When eventually he phones, we refuse to speak to him.

C) In an epiphany of insight, Nicolas Cage recognises that the crop circles are the most important thing on the planet. He races off to meetings with his studio, his lawyer, his agent, his trainer, to put his considerable weight behind a crop circle blockbuster. The calendar is left behind to put us off the scent.

D) The fat biker is really Steven Spielberg in disguise. He rolls up the calendar and sticks it up his sweatshirt. He races to meetings with his studio, his lawyer, his agent, his trainer, to put his considerable weight behind a crop circle blockbuster.

As circumstances unfold, I must assure you, dear reader, that you, not the *Hollywood Reporter*, will be the first to know.

But now, a deliberate mistake. I was trying to catch you out – checking to make sure you were attending. Hypothesis D above is impossible. If the calendar was left behind, how could the fat biker/

Steven Spielberg have stuck it up his sweatshirt? Ha.

* * * * *

Something of real significance has happened. Hands across the Cs!

It seems to be a given that crop circle activity is centred in Wessex but that they occur in many other countries. What has seemed to elude us is evidence of common authorship or a stylistic link. The non-English formations remind us, year-by-year, of design themes that were explored three or four years previously in Wiltshire and Hampshire. Occasionally, as in the wonderful Nemilkov, Czech Republic formation of two years ago or Drieschor, Holland, last year, there is an approach to a tentative link to current English circles.

America has long exhibited what appears to be apprentice works. Formal ideas which were explored in depth in England some years ago were rehearsed – rather scrappily – in America. There was never any doubt that US circles were improving but I have been searching for some years for evidence that they were made by the same authors as the English ones.

In early June last summer a formation appeared in Salem, Oregon. It arrived on the land of farmer Wavra who was generally sympathetic but naturally anxious about unannounced public visits. The pattern is impressive for its clean graphic quality. An early visitor likened it to "two horseshoes", a letter C inside a larger letter C. This impression is confirmed by the positioning of the formation. If north is 'up' the Cs are in the correct orientation. What might CC stand for, I ask myself?

The outer laid ring was anticlockwise, the inner clockwise and the central circle was anticlockwise. This, in itself, indicates a certain sophistication. However, a striking and unusual feature was the rather fleshy tendril to the east, like an extroverted belly button.

All the visitors noted it and said that it seemed to be a deliberate and important part of the design.

The meaning of this tendril did not become clear until the West Clandon pictogram of about 9th August 1997 appeared. On close examination – in fact on the most superficial examination – it was apparent that the two 'hands' on the eastern and western extremities were identical 'CC' replicas of the Oregon formation. Not similar, but identical. This, I believe, is the first occasion in the history of this bewildering phenomenon that we have seen such a specific formal link between the US and UK formations. Perhaps the fleshy appendage was indicating "Watch this space, I am growing".

* * * * *

There is a very important distinction between a maze and a labyrinth. A labyrinth is unicursal, that is it has a single path which goes, normally, from the outside to the centre. One cannot get lost in a labyrinth. A maze, on the other hand, offers many routes, some of which lead nowhere and thus activates the left reasoning brain. The function of a maze is to lose you. Mazes, being concerned with reasoning, are never sacred. Labyrinths, which offer no choices but encourage a contemplative state of mind, are often associated with the sacred and some are actually incorporated into churches, the most famous being the 11 ring Labyrinth laid into the floor at Chartres Cathedral.

This duality is important as – while mazes have occasionally occurred in the circles – the spirit of the labyrinth is often more apparent.

What might this have to do with the circles? Well, like everything, these ideas can only be tentative. I offer no more than a hypothesis, but it seems to work. The Circlemakers appear to have many agendas, but among these, two stand out.

First, the respect for life. They never destroy the plant and, with the exception of the two unhappy Canadian porcupines, they have never hurt anything. Second, hospitality. An inhospitable formation has never manifested. The tramlines (for so long the "evidence" for hoaxing) lead us ceremonially in and gateway openings are always left so that we do not trample crop down. This can be construed as Labyrinthine in nature. Of course, it might be argued that these two policies are essentially incompatible. The simple act of walking in a circle at least modifies the life of the crop.

Now clearly, crop circles do not offer a single winding path, though they occasionally have. They do, however, always offer clues as to how they might be walked. The direction of the lay of the crop is almost as powerful a signal as big arrows painted on the ground. Walking against the flow is uncomfortable at many levels. A turn in direction of lay is an almost undeniable invitation to follow.

All of this becomes closer and more tangible if shoes are removed. But above all, the central lesson of the circles when you enter is Look! Listen!

* * * * *

Now Sacred Geometry. If Geometry is concerned essentially with the measure of the Earth, Sacred Geometry could be, as Robert Lawlor has called it, a metaphor of "Universal Order".

The Division of Unity is the primal act of Sacred Geometry. Lawlor again: "Those who use geometric figures to describe the beginning of Creation must attempt to show how an absolute Unity can become multiplicity and diversity. "

The circle is a shape dear to the hearts of many people. For some cultures it is a mystical symbol and for many it is a symbol of God, of the Universe or of the Spiritual. It has been said that it represents a God whose centre is everywhere and whose perimeter is nowhere. How – in order to symbolise the transition from Unity to Manifestation – might we divide it?

The Vesica Pisces is the classic symbol of the Division of Unity. The centre of each of the two circles is positioned on the perimeter of the other. This juxtaposition creates the almond-shaped Vesica which precisely contains two equilateral triangles. This diagram is the basis for many geometries including the Flower of Life, which appeared, subtly adapted, as a formation in Froxfield in 1994. The widespread belief that the central element, the almond or eye, fits inside a Golden Section rectangle (1:1.618) is simply wrong. It is a 1:1.732 proportion, the square root of 3.

In 1996 we were given an unmistakable Vesica Pisces formation at Ashbury. But while there can be no mistake about what it symbolised – the Primal act of Sacred Geometry – close observation reveals a subtle modification; gaps at the positions where the crescents classically connect. This is where the Labyrinth returns. If the diagram had been meticulously duplicated, visitors would have had to stomp the wheat down to enter the central space. By separating the crescents slightly gateways are offered to us. The life of the wheat is respected and hospitality to visitors is asserted.

* * * * *

Now comfortably settled in Wiltshire for the season, I was shocked to hear (for it was late and I was about to go to bed) a gentle knock on the door. Curious, I opened it to find two white-clad ladies.

"Are you Michael?" they asked, a surname seeming unnecessary. I confirmed that I was and invited them in. I was struck immediately by their elegance and gentleness. They appeared to glow. Their faces seemed to be illuminated by private spotlights. Their hands were particularly graceful.

Women in White: "We thought we should speak to you at the start of this season. Something wonderful is going to happen."

MG: "But something wonderful happens every season...."

WIW: "Yes, but this will be extraordinary."

MG: "Well, OK. But forgive me for asking. Just who are you?"

WIW: "We are responsible for the circles."

MG: "Oh, come on. I had the impression that you were a couple of girls from The Barge campground."

WIW: "Oh, no! We are representatives of the CFC, the Cosmic Federation of Circlemanifestors. We are in the design department and we have been put in charge of the Innovation Programme."

MG: "Innovation Programme? Everything you guys...er, people.... do seems to be innovative."

WIW: "Yes, we're rather proud of what we have achieved so far but there is pressure from upstairs to do even better. "Make it grate in '98" is our new slogan. We've had a couple of ideas which we think you are all going to enjoy this year. We'll be doing a test-run in a couple of weeks and we'll watch your reaction."

MG: "So you are designers?"

WIW1: "I suppose in your civilisation "designer" would be an appropriate word, but we think of ourselves more as developmental therapists..."

WIW2: "...or transformational magicians."

WIW: "...or draftspersons of metamorphosis, perhaps."

MG: "Well, it is very kind of you to visit me and keep me up to date. Is there anything you would like me to do?"

WIW: "Watch this space. Or rather, these spaces. We are Cleo and Persephone, by the way."

There was a brief flash of intense lime-green light which filled the whole room and they simply were no longer there.

* * * * *

"Which is your favourite formation?", people sometimes ask and while for years I have avoided this almost impossible dilemma, I suppose that it must be for me, the Bythorn Mandala of 1993.

It was little visited but somehow I was lucky enough to see it three times, and on one occasion I helped measure it. Five years later I find that I am still preoccupied with the implications of this majestic formation. It continues, in small steps, to reveal itself. Imagine my delight when I went into the new Avebury Trusloe pentagram a few days ago and found that it was a precisely formed sister of Bythorn.

Not a replica. A sibling.

It has the five-pointed star and the ten surrounding petals. It has a complex and articulate lay. Most touching of all (for me at least) is the fact that it meticulously obeys the rules set for pentagrams by the big sister Bythorn: it points south.

There have only been three manifested pentagrams though they are often there as hidden proportional constraints. The second was Bishops Cannings last year which also pointed south.

* * * * *

Please do not write to me about the visit of the Women in White. I must make it clear that this section was made up, invented, a work of the imagination. It is not true. It did not happen. I was not visited by anyone, nor, under the circumstances, was I able to tape the conversation or to take photographs. Small tissue samples were not taken from the flesh of their calves and I did not examine the irises of their eyes in any detail

* * * * *

Living in Wiltshire for the past few summers, it is impossible not to notice the massive concentration of armaments to the south. Salisbury Plain must be one of the biggest arms dumps in England, if not Europe. Many of the roads are marked with stocky yellow posts and signs saying "Tank crossing." The dull thud of explosives is a familiar part of the day. Last year, before another tinpot expedition to the Middle East or somewhere, fighter pilots were flying so low that the eardrums of everyone between Devizes and Marlborough were put at risk. What an irony! What seems to be the gentlest and most spirit-enhancing of phenomena positions itself a few miles away from this garbage. Here, perhaps, is another lesson. (Ironically, as I write this, I can hear the sound of artillery fire.)

One evening, trying to sleep, I counted five helicopters. Of course, it could have been one passing repeatedly specifically to keep me awake, but it does make you wonder what exactly they are doing. There are numerous reports of luminosity pursuits by military helicopters, marked and unmarked, this year and this raises many questions. Observation from the field repeatedly indicates that the luminosities are nimble and evasive. They simply blink out when it suits them. Why then does the military continue what seems to be a doomed enterprise and how do they know they are there? If, which I doubt, they can be seen on radar, how are the helicopters scrambled within the very short time the luminosities usually appear?

* * * * *

Farmers' dramas. I have been thrown out of a field. This is the first time this has happened to me. I had been told (and believed) that a general permission had been obtained. The farmer, or more accurately in this case, the estate manager, softened when we were all out and told us how poor the crop is this year. He expressed his resentment of the "vandals" who continue to make the formations and compared their work to graffiti in cities. It would have been churlish to interrupt him to say that very few formations were hoaxes and that his certainly was not. We listened respectfully until he finished.

The farmer with the large ring formation at Avebury refused access to anyone and said he was going to bring in the combine and cut it out immediately. (This reminds me of the old Mafia dictum that guns should be kept out of sight until they are ready for use. It is unwise to disclose intentions.) I believe the formation is still there as I write days later.

The farmer at Dadford, near Silverstone, was moaning because he was certain that his magnificent double pentagram had been made by kids. Of course he had never seen it and, when shown the photograph he was overwhelmed. A few days later he was taught to dowse by an American lady dowser. Another life changed. Another raft of certainties sunk forever.

Polly Carson, who this year was hostess to the huge seven-fold figure in the East Field at Alton Barnes is charmed and feels that she has, again received a blessing. It was, it should be pointed out, a 1.6 acre blessing involving at least four tons of laid wheat. And there are still 'researchers' out there who insist it was man made. The Delusional Cultist wing of crop circle studies goes from strength to strength.

* * * * *

This has been the most articulate season we have ever experienced. Certainly the geometric implications have been astonishing. To date we have seen a real development of five-fold geometry with the Beckhampton pentagram and then the Dadford double pentagram, the double Vesica, in the negative on the A4 at Clatford and the positive at Furze Hill and then, for the first time, the arrival of seven-fold at Alton Barnes and at Danebury. Five-fold is the geometry of life. Seven-fold is the geometry of revelation and spirit. I have been waiting for it for years. The gigantic 50p piece in East Field is a real treat. As I write, another, more advanced version has appeared at Tawsmead Copse.

*****

Looking back to the heady delights of 1990 (the arrival of the straight line) and the bewilderments of early 1991 (insectograms, dolphins, keys and, above all, the miraculous Barbury Castle), we were stunned by the 1991 Ickleton Mandelbrot. A beautifully made and totally assured formation visited by just a handful of people.

Even fewer of us knew who Benoit Mandelbrot was and what 'fractal' meant but we all suspected that it was important. Copies of Gleick's book *Chaos* were bought and read and those of us who, in those early days, had access to a computer installed the relevant programme and watched as, no matter how you shrank it or enlarged it, the familiar cardioid shape reappeared.

Whether or not the formation was a perfect Mandelbrot set or instead an accurate simulation of one was the cause of some debate, but since that time the word 'fractal' has become a part of the croppie vocabulary. For us it has simply come to mean an elaborate shape with self-similarity created by lots of small circles. Who would argue with that

In 1996 vast 'Julia set' fractals appeared at Windmill Hill and beside Stonehenge (Julia sets are, apparently, detailed investigations of specific areas of the Mandelbrot set). Then, the following year formations at Silbury Hill and Milk Hill conformed precisely to another type of fractal protocol – the Koch snowflake, which, simply put, is as follows:

Take an equilateral triangle and divide each side into three equal sections. Place a smaller equilateral (one third the original size) at the centre of each original side. Repeat the system on each of the twelve equal surfaces thus created. Continue ad infinitum. And it is perhaps the "ad infinitum" which makes the Koch protocol so thrilling.

84

Theoretically, this system could go on forever, increasing the length of its perimeter infinitely – literally infinitely – while never significantly enlarging its real area. Koch thus can be seen as a container of enormous symbolism.

The original Silbury Hill fractal was repeated at Milk Hill, this time with what could only be seen as an inverted Koch fractal at its centre. While the outer forms developed outward, the inner form at Milk Hill ate itself and grew inward. I believe this was the first time this had been seen.

And so to this season. Following the initial lovely seven-fold at Danebury we got the giant heptagon at East Field. (Two things: first, this was, at 1.6 acres, or 6000 square metres, the biggest single area of laid crop we have ever had. Second, we see a repeat of a previous Alton Barnes trait. East Field has twice, in 1991 and now 1998, hosted not the first formation of a new type but the second.)

East Field and its sister formation at Tawsmead Copse represent in many ways a parallel to the Silbury/Milk Hill formations. The former has a huge uninterrupted central area and the second contains a central flower, but here the similarities end.

East Field and Tawsmead were certainly not snowflakes.

1999

The problem with much of the debunkers literature is basically a lack of lightness, humour or irony. How can one claim to be interested in the circles and be so miserable and – dare I say it – so embittered? However, I was sent a Xerox of a page in which 'K. Short' suggests that in my Alton Barnes Crop Circle Celebration talk last year I was egocentric and patronising and aspired to the mantle of guruism! In addition he feels that I talked down to my audience, addressing them like children. I am sure that 'K.', if I may call him that, writes with only the most pure of motives and I am grateful for his observations. Last year I was a only a Delusional Cultist. I must try harder.

* * * * *

I went up to Vancouver to talk to UFO*BC (British Columbia, not Before Christ!). I am always hesitant about UFO groups. Their world view is often so locked into an almost McCarthyite invasion-paranoia that they cannot bear to hear of a phenomenon with no dark side, no abductions, mutilations, cover-ups or CIA involvement. BC was delightfully different and question time continued until we were, literally, asked to leave by a lady in uniform who started to switch the lights off.

I stayed with Chad and Gwen Deetken, Canadian stalwarts of crop circle research. (For the first time in years, Chad was not in England last season. With the benefit of hindsight, it was probably a blessing. He would certainly have taken a baseball bat to certain 'artists' and would be in prison now for Grievous Bodily Harm.)

Chad had just finished reading *Alternative Science* by Richard Milton and a few days after my return he sent me a copy. This is one of the most impressive and thoughtful books I have read and I believe it to be an absolutely essential read for anyone interested in the circles and indeed for anyone interested in the world. It calmly and carefully analyses modern scientific and medical practice and, with a wealth of cited evidence, exposes modern scientism as the fundamentalism it has become. It shows how the technical benefits of our time have largely arisen from individual initiative in spite of scientific consensus. For crop circle research, though the circles are mentioned only once, it confirms that any reconciliation with conventional science is impossible. Please read it.

* * * * *

Predictions are always dangerous and demonstrate the egocentric side of one's character. Season by season I have tried to side-step this issue but the arrival last season of sevenfold geometry which I had been awaiting for several years has emboldened me to further stick my neck out. What we saw was essentially heptagon-based. That is, we had seven-sided figures but not seven-pointed. Yet. I suggest the geometric progress of seven is from the Heptagon (which we have had) through the Fat Heptagram to the Thin Heptagram. Prediction One is a Fat Heptagram.

Prediction Two is the manifestation of the Geometry of Eleven. I believe that eleven is the second complex number, the second Labyrinth number, and will show us the geometry of Unfoldment. In the amazing Stonehenge spiral of 1996, Circle 22 played a crucial role. When aligned through the large central circle, Circle 1, they pointed north. The lovely 'Beltane wheel' ring in Canola at Silbury last May had 33 circles and the huge disc at Avebury was based on elevenfold proportion. Perhaps something is being telegraphed here.

Would it be patronising to mention that the area of a Heptagon can be found by using the formula $3.6339n$ and that of an Undecagon (eleven sided) by the formula $9.3565n$ where n is side length?

* * * * *

The arrival last year of sevenfold geometry also brought up the question of the 1990 Bickington, Devon, formation. This had seven satellites and seemed to challenge Danebury for the First Sevenfold Cup. I dug deep into my archive and found a very accurate survey by Barbara Davies, who was for many years one of the true stalwarts of crop circle research. The survey is a meticulous study which takes compass bearings to every point and so I now have "conclusive evidence" (as others are fond of saying) that this was not a sevenfold.

Satellites 2, 4, 6 & 8 conformed to classic quintuplet geometry. These four circles are disposed on a substantially right-angle grid, the angles between them being 98°, 85°, 95° and 82° respectively. Satellites 3,5 & 7 were additions to the classic quintuplet design. Thus, though the formation had seven satellites it was clearly not Sevenfold as they were not evenly placed around the formation at a series of 51. 4...° angles.

* * * * *

In the real world, confessions carry a great weight. They are often interpreted as moments of epiphany, of cleansing, of squaring of accounts. This, of course, must take into account the fact that a confession, in the real world, is not to be taken lightly.

The confessor will face sanctions, ranging from social discomfort for slight infractions to imprisonment for crimes. Confessions do not come easy. The reward for truth is often outweighed by the gravity of the punishment.

But we are not in the real world. Around the crop circles everything is reversed. Crop circle confessors are not liable for punishment; they are more likely to receive rewards, even if those rewards are the satisfaction of their own nature. They have learned that the farmers, despite their protestations, will never press criminal charges and the National Farmers Union, despite their offer of a £10,000 reward, will never follow leads.

I remember a certain hoax claimant letting slip to a group of us that the major satisfaction he got from his activity was the embarrassment and discomfiture of those he misled. Ah, history! Tragically, we have learned nothing. Was there ever a single crop circle confession which was shown to be true? Well, no. Were there confessions which were clearly false? Yes, the majority. Have we learned to exercise our experience, judgement and discernment in this area? Clearly not.

* * * * *

In Walt Disney's *Snow White and the Seven Dwarves*, the wicked queen is peeved because Snow White is more beautiful than she is. She hires a huntsman to kill Snow White in the forest and, the job purportedly done, he brings the evil queen a heart, claiming it belonged to the pretty girl. "Mirror, mirror on the wall. Who is the fairest of them all?" asks the vain and nasty queen, certain (after her monstrous deed) of the answer she will get.

To her anger, the mirror responds, "Snow White's the fairest in the land. You hold a pig's heart in your hand."

"A pig's heart!" cries her majesty, who clearly did not take a degree in forensic pathology, "I've been tricked!"

I am glad to be running towards the future with my arms open. Of course there is a risk that I will trip and fall flat on my face. Far better than leaning over backwards to avoid change, firmly grasping a pig's heart.

* * * * *

In a recent letter Dudley Young asked where the meanings I attributed to numbers and geometry came from. He went on to talk about an article in *Steamhovel Press*, concluding "Sacred Geometry or just loony crap?" I will ignore this pithy assessment and assume he truly wants to know. I am grateful for his question. It has concentrated my mind. I have given it serious thought for some weeks and consulted fairly widely on the subject. One authority I asked about this replied "There's no disagreement on this subject – our understanding of the meaning of number originates with Nature, and – subject to reinterpretation by scholars over the centuries – there is a consensus". Another scholar in the field, John Michell, however, while broadly accepting the consensus, feels that interpretation can be modified by individual study. For example, he asks, how can a number be given to God?

The circle, a one-sided figure, is the symbol of 1. Ancient mathematicians referred to 1, The Monad, as The First, The Seed, The Essence. Others feel that it represents God, Unity, All-that-Is.

2, The Dyad, is often seen to represent "that which is Other". The Division of Unity, the first act of Sacred Geometry, elegantly divides the prime Circle by the use of the Vesica Pisces. The two-sided Vesica, shaped like an almond, is the symbol of two.

3, The Triad, is obviously represented by a triangle, classically an equilateral. Three can be seen as the first step in unfoldment or, as some prefer, completion. As the first child of the Monad and the Dyad, it can be seen as containing all possibility.

4, The Tetrad is clearly embodied in the square. The Tetrad is often seen to be the first movement from two dimensionality (the triangle) into three dimensions, the tetrahedron which has four surfaces. It is the number of Experience, of Materiality, of Substance. Many consider the square and four as symbolic of the World.

5, The Pentad, is represented by the pentagram, the five-pointed star, and is associated with life itself. The Pentagram contains the Golden Section, a proportion widely present in living forms, not least our own. It has been adopted as a symbol for Magic and also, more recently, for several countries and companies.

The shape of 6, the Hexad, is logically the Hexagon. Certain commentators feel that the progress through the numbers has now achieved Structure, Function and order which six represents. Others argue that six is the Crystalline or mineral aspect of Earth.

7, The Heptad, is known as the Virgin, because of the number's resistance to combining with other numbers. It is said to have great magical and mystical power and is the number of Spirit and Revelation.

Having passed the Virgin, we come to 8, the Octad, which unlike its predecessor combines promiscuously with almost everything. The ancients called eight justice. Eight, uniquely, can be halved all the way back to unity.

9, The Nonagon, is made most powerful by its association with three. It is composed of three trinities and in some cultures was considered thrice sacred.

10, The Decad, is considered an aspect of 1, the Monad. 10 also represents a balanced form of life, 5 doubled. If 1 and 2 are seen as the mother and father of all numbers, then perhaps 3 to 9 can be considered their children, each with a different character. With the arrival of 10, the first double digit number, all possibilities become available. 1 and 0 can be construed as symbols of genitals. The digital revolution is based on them.

Number in our society is simply for counting things while the beautiful younger sister, Geometry, now helps us to design objects. In other times, both of these disciplines carried a heavy freight of meaning and symbolism which is now largely lost to us.

Should anyone wish to pursue this subject further they should contact me and I will suggest some references.

* * * * *

This season promises us the hilarious spectacle of the monstrous affiliation of money and science reducing crop circle research to the status of a criminal investigation. I am sure you would not expect me to comment further! The really important news is the arrival of the beautiful 'Menorah' formation at Barbury Castle. Clearly this area is making a concerted bid at becoming the venue for Jewish Mysticism. The numbers are important here. The figure contains 11 circles (I told you 11 would come). The 11 is made up of seven horizontals ('candles') and four down the stem. I believe it tells of the reconciliation of Spirit with the World. We will receive many fours and squares this summer.

* * * * *

I spend too much time dealing with the antics of the hoax claimants and I resent every second I give to the subject. It is entirely without profit and it demeans us all. We are involved in a high work and these villains repeatedly and fraudulently succeed in getting our attention.

An interesting argument against ignoring them is the regrettable fact that they leave a huge volume of hypocrisy behind them. Someone has to clean up! Here in the US, for example, the original Doug and Dave footage is played relentlessly and – inevitably – it has an effect. People actually believe this stuff. What is one to do? It's a rotten job but someone must clean up the sewage.

In all their claims during the last ten years (the whole ever-changing unpleasant cast from D & D to the unappetising 'Team Satan'), we never hear a note of artistic pride. They are very pleased with their supposed mechanical skills and their superlative PR. Above all, like disturbed adolescents, they take real pleasure in cheating. Their highest aspiration is deceit and the discomfiture it causes. However, when have they spoken with warmth or understanding about their claimed achievement? In 10 years I do not recollect a single occasion. And now, when the current members of this shifting, ephemeral crew call themselves artists, we might have expected, just occasionally, a note of pride in this prodigious art which they call their own. Don't hold your breath!

Interviewer: "Mr. Scorsese, people have been, as usual, very moved by your latest work. Can you comment?"

Martin Scorsese: "I was very pleased that it was in focus all the way through."

Interviewer: "Herr Mozart, your latest quartets are divine. What can you tell us?"

Mozart: "The musicians were all in tune."

Interviewer: "Mr. Rembrandt, your paintings are said to establish new standards. How do you respond to the public's appreciation?"

Rembrandt: "There was very little paint dripped on the floor."

* * * * *

Many readers will have heard of this season's video footage of luminosities over several formations. I have received a letter from professor Anthony Antennae of the Department of Lepidoptery (the study of butterflies) at the University of Creepy, Crawley, who points out that, having examined all this year's footage and that of previous years that the luminosities are all, in fact, butterflies. There are three types of white butterfly found in this area during the summer, the Small Cabbage White, the Large Cabbage White and the Greenveined White. Professor Antennae confirms that every supposed luminosity every filmed is in fact one of these.

Contradicting this conclusion is the evidence of several witnesses to events overlooking the Oliver's Castle formation. A party of Japanese visitors were seen on the hill rapidly making small Origami birds or gliders out of brilliant white paper. These were then passed to a group of Chinese Tai Chi Masters, under the direction of Dr. Nan Lu, who, with astonishing power and slow control, threw them into the air to glide gently, before the unwitting videographers, over the formation. My case rests.

This summer also brought hard technical support for the Oliver's Castle balls of light footage in the form of video analysis by Chris Everard which demonstrated other areas of mysterious light activity on the periphery of the screen. This was never mentioned by either the supposed hoaxer or his supporters. The Everard work is, to use one of the favoured phrases of the last few years "the final nail in the coffin" of the faked tape nonsense.

2000

I write this in the first of the 21st Century, in Alton Barnes. I have returned to live in England and hope to spend the next hundred years or so in Wiltshire, close to the heart of this phenomenon which has moved so many of us.

I had forgotten just how noisy those silly soldiers on Salisbury Plain can be. The sound of enormous explosions and astonishing bombardments are a counterpoint to the racket of low-flying military planes. It is remarkable that here, where we can witness the most mysterious, beautiful and optimistic events on the surface of the planet, we are within earshot of madness and destruction. I suppose it serves to remind us that on Planet Earth, we have choice. We are free to think or believe whatever we might wish.

The truth is like a cork in the ocean. No matter how hard you try to hold it down, it must eventually bob to the surface.

* * * * *

Few generations have lived through the passage between millennia and, some weeks after zero hour, there are compelling lessons for us all. There was, in America at least, a powerful industry set up to scare us. There would be no food or water, domestic energy supply would break down while petrol would be unavailable. Citizens should either head for the hills or arm themselves to protect their families against marauders. Roads would be blocked and airliners would plunge from the skies like zapped fruit-flies. In the event it was a hollow fraud, but hundreds of bewildered (and over-stocked) paranoiacs are now seriously considering their future. There were no apologies and nor will there be.

Like little kids desperate for frightening stories, we always seem to swallow it and, I suppose, our need to be scared is so fundamental a human urge that the tellers of fearful tales, the weavers of utterly hollow paranoias, the inventors of scary myths, will always find a willing audience. Crop circle students might bear this in mind.

* * * * *

Like many of us, I find that this small area of Wiltshire has become, through our summer visits, remarkably familiar. It has taken on the comfortable outlines of dearly-loved childhood holiday places. Every road passes by fields which have been the site of significant and magical formations or memorable gatherings. Each field seems to carry a message.

I have visited in winter but never lived here. The green or gold is comprehensively replaced – in the morning at least – with the white of vigorous frost, like powdered sugar. It melts off by lunchtime. This week Silbury Hill was virtually encircled by a frozen moat. And there was a Millennial surprise from Devizes Town Council! A new white horse, the eighth, has been cut into the hill overlooking Roundway.

The fields are pregnant. We are in for another amazing year.

* * * * *

Since I arrived in this magical landscape, I have seen three deer, frozen for a moment in the beam of my headlights. They recovered quickly and leaped through the hedgerow into the field. The next day, driving along the lovely valley between Devizes and Beckhampton which has held so many crop formations, I saw two bison grazing at Baltic Farm. I was late and had to hurry by. I returned in excitement a couple of times, but they were never there. And then, of course, logic kicks in. There cannot be buffalo in Wiltshire! This is impossible. They must have been a couple of hoaxed Highland Cattle. Much more reasonable.

* * * * *

Anticipating the coming season, it seems appropriate to contemplate what might be the trajectory of this phenomenon and to speculate on some of the themes it might pursue.

We can begin with the geometry of the five pointed star, the pentagram, which has been explored over the past years. Important work at the start of the '90s showed that a pentagram (a form which contains the Golden Section proportion) was invisibly present as a guiding constraint in many of the early formations. Though it was so widespread as a hidden skeleton, the pentagram itself never appeared until Bythorn in 1993. There have been several pentagrams since then, but the pentagon, the five-sided figure, has always featured only as a supporting form. So prediction 1 is a pentagon in its own right.

The Seven, by contrast, has been represented only by Heptagons, or forms based on the Heptagon, a seven sided figure. Prediction 2 is a

Heptagram, a seven-pointed star.

Last year I suggested eleven would arrive. I was thinking, I admit, of the geometry of eleven and I was wrong. We didn't get it. However, we had a couple of formations in which the number eleven was crucial, the Barbury Castle Menorah and the Devil's Den formation. Prediction 3, then, is eleven-fold geometry.

Finally, and with no more evidence than my intuition, I believe that the 2000 season will include reference (although preliminary) to 13, the number of Transformation.

If these shapes appear, I will be delighted. It will be a confirmation of the validity of certain ideas. If they do not appear, I will not open my veins in public, nor will I petulantly announce my retirement.

* * * * *

I promised not to reveal this earlier, but I can now report that Elvis was seen, by several reliable and independent witnesses, in a crop circle last year. Mr. and Mrs. Charles Kreuzer of Kansas City woke early to go to the Cherhill formation. When they got there, they saw a black stretch limo with darkened windows by the roadside. There were several suited individuals who prevented them from entering the field. A little while later, Joseph Trellis and his girlfriend Christine Haythorne, both of Lincolnshire, arrived and were also told that they would have to wait. The four visitors moved down the road to a vantage point from where they observed the circle through Mr. Kreuzer's binoculars. They saw a rather paunchy, long-haired individual in sun-glasses and a white sequinned jump-suit with flare bottoms. There were several other dark-suited minders guarding the perimeter of the formation and peering cautiously outwards.

Suddenly the party decided to leave the formation. They returned to the road at what Mr. Kreuzer, a former marine, described as "a trot". "It looked to me like Elvis was being carried," he said. The limousine and two accompanying cars left at speed towards Beckhampton.

It is encouraging to know that at least one member of the Presley family is truly interested in the circles.

* * * * *

"Welcome to planet Maturia! We have much to teach you." says Lisa Kudrow in *The Opposite of Sex*.

The last few years have convinced me that the human mind is the loveliest and most whimsical, most inventive and funny, the most poetic and wise thing we know in the whole Universe (so far!). Not surprising then that I am driven so regularly to despair by people's refusal to use the dynamo we all own. A user's manual should be available. I am not speaking here of intelligence or the lack of it, or of education (or the lack of it), but of simple, sequential, logical common sense.

'Ratiocination' is a useful word here. The ability to reason or to go through logical processes. You do not have to be Albert Einstein to realise that the banging of heads against walls brings pain. We all soon learn not to bang our head.

During lectures or radio programmes in America there were often call-ins offering another "solution" to the crop circle mystery. It was simple! They were caused by laser beams directed from Pentagon controlled satellites. Dozens of people across the US had come to the same blinding recognition, and having gained real comfort from the realisation that this unknown (i.e. threatening) mystery could be laid at the door of the army (i.e. comfortable authority), they could go to sleep.

I asked them to pursue their own idea to its conclusion. First, what was the use of a weapons system that elegantly bent crop? Second, why was it being shown in public? Third, why was it being demonstrated on the farmland of another nation state? Fourth, how had they got Leonardo da Vinci to work for them? None of these questions, of course, address the technical questions. How do you precisely stabilise the platform (the satellite) at the moment of activation to eliminate "smudging"? How do you deal with the great weight of the power source that would be needed for such a laser? A satellite expert once confirmed to me that current conventional technology, at least, has no answers to these questions.

Another example. Recently a young man driving by Silbury Hill in the early hours of the morning saw a ring of coloured lights suspended over the hill. It was reported, sympathetically, by the local Devizes paper and, of course, by the following issue the explanologists were in full flood with their wacky solutions. The most interesting was that this was caused by poachers hunting hares who had fixed lights to a large wooden frame and taken it to the top of the hill.

OK. Hares on top of Silbury Hill? Multi-coloured lights? The effort of heaving this imagined device up the precarious path? In the dark? And the weight of the batteries? But I am sure that the culprit was pleased to get his dumb notion printed.

* * * * *

The oilseed rape is nearly three feet tall and is starting to blossom, I notice something I have never seen before. When the field slopes, the flowers bloom first at the bottom of the hill, leaving the upper reaches green. My tentative guess is that there is more moisture lower down but, whatever, it looks lovely, like a watercolour where the saturated pigment runs to the bottom of the paper.

* * * * *

Looking over the history of the past few years, I sense a movement towards webs, meshes, knots and weaves. Last year, at Stanton St. Bernard, we had a delicately interwoven knot, very similar to that illustrated in the 'Book of Kells' and, of course, the season ended with the astonishing 7-fold "basket". In the first case the weaving was graphically expressed in the design while in the second the crop itself was woven.

Just as we seem to get better, year by year, in dealing with the circles, is it unreasonable to speculate that perhaps the circlemakers might become more adept as the seasons go by? Certainly they seemed to demonstrate a couple of new skills last year.

* * * * *

I am aware that my frequent railings (or perhaps snipings would be a better word) against the noisy games of her Majesty's army can upset some readers, so I promise never ever to mention it again. (Unless they mistakenly nuke Devizes as part of their "Manoeuvres".)

Salisbury Plain seems to have acquired a new – even bigger – piece of artillery, and our boys simply love playing with it. In my innocent way, I thought the bangs we had been hearing were as loud as anyone could need but, in the last few weeks, the relentless wallops literally shake the windows of hapless local residents (like me). A local church reportedly had a large picture fall off the wall. Still, we shouldn't moan. It is reassuring to know that we can quickly see off those Serbs/ Iraqis/ Argentinians/ Gypsies/ Unmarried Mothers/ Bogus Asylum Seekers or whoever this week's enemy happens to be.

I heard on the news, and I swear this is true, that the Navy, hoping to save money, have decided not to use real shells in their firing practice. Their shells cost £649 a pop, which I assume to be peanuts when compared with the megatonnage they use on the Plain. Navy gunners (please believe me) are now using blanks and are expected to say "Bang" when they pull the string.

* * * * *

This is an unusual season. The weather through April and May was awful, and though we know that the circles appear whenever they wish, an air of courageous acceptance seemed to descend. "We are in for a slow season," people said, adding like brave little soldiers (see above) "But of course it doesn't matter! Whatever we get will be welcome."

But on 18th June, a remarkable formation appeared at Windmill Hill which was the most assured graphic expression of three-dimensionality that the circles have ever demonstrated. On the same day, on Bishop's Cannings Down, another 3-D formation appeared. In this case, standard perspective drawing was employed rather than the Windmill Hill Op-art. But they were both totally incomprehensible from the ground. Aerial photographs, or accurate drawings showed an implied solidity that we had never seen before. Bishops Cannings might be viewed as three starfish clinging to a grapefruit. Two of the legs (arms? limbs? appendages?) of each disappear around the back of the sphere while the central leg in the foreground is gracefully angled sideways into an exquisite composition.

The beautiful South Field formation did not aspire to the solidity of its siblings, but it had other delightful features. The sixteen spokes which separated the radial leaves narrowed as they swept inwards. They converged to the centre with a precision which I had never witnessed before.

* * * * *

One of the people who are taken in by the lies of the so-called hoaxers is Farmer Naughton of Bishops Cannings, who last year brought his combine to cut out the lovely seven-fold 'basket' rather than leave it for people to enjoy. This year, to the astonishment of all, he put up an honesty box and opened the field.

I visited him to thank him and to take him a photograph and drawing of his new formation, which to me is one of the most articulate geometrical designs we have ever had. He said that he had wanted to cut it out immediately, but his wife persuaded him, against his better judgement, to allow people in.

He glanced at the picture, but was anxious to let me know that he still thought it was done by vandals. I suggested then that he and I go immediately half a mile down the road to the Wiltshire Constabulary Headquarters. We could ask why, as predictable acts of damage to property take place every year in a limited area and within a defined season, they have never made an arrest. I told him that I was able to supply the names both of individuals who claim to cause this damage and "researchers" who aid and promote them.

He was not too keen on that idea. I wonder why not? A few days later, the circlemakers, to reward him I guess, delivered another formation into the same field. He was not delighted.

* * * * *

While Janet Ossebaard stood taking photographs at Alton Priors, a car drew up beside her. "Janet, Janet," said Matthew Williams, the amateur hoax claimant (for it was he), "I want to show you something. "

Janet, wishing to leave as quickly as possible, muttered something about needing to get away, but our Matt, showing both the insensitivity and persistence which have endeared him to so many, insisted.

"This won't take a minute," he said portentously, deftly unlocking the car boot. The lid opened to reveal a plank of wood wrapped in black plastic tape, "Hoaxing equipment!" he said with the air of one revealing the secret of the Universe. Janet, deeply worried about the poor man's mental health, hurried away.

Discuss this episode briefly (it's really not worth more than a few words) in terms of:

a) Social dysfunction
b) Psycho-sexual symbolism
c) Rural petty criminals
d) Desperate boredom among the unemployed
e) Evidence of attention-starvation during childhood.

* * * * *

"Today I settle all family business, so don't tell me you're innocent." Al Pacino, Michael Corleone in *The Godfather*.

The last few weeks have been difficult for me. The messages from friends and well-wishers gently drawing my attention to my numerous failures and inadequacies have been overwhelming. Under this barrage from sincere and selfless colleagues (and, oh, how can I ever thank you all), I have had to reassess my behaviour. It seems appropriate now to confess my sins and inexcusable activities. I list the accusations in order.

1. Michael Glickman believes all crop circles are real.

They have uncovered my guilty secret! I know that ALL crop circles are hoaxed and I have always known it. I lied and I got, I must admit, a sick thrill every time you all fell for it. Dr. Colin Andrews, the scientist, in his estimate of 80% man-made fell far short of the reality. For years I have hoodwinked the public with my writing and lectures, deluding everyone into believing all that woo-woo, New Agey spirituality nonsense. Geometry? Design? Proportion? Number? – Baloney!

2. Michael Glickman is part of the Crop Circle Industry but really he knows the truth.

Again I have to thank Dr. Andrews for blowing the whistle on the Crop Circle Industry and I must abjectly confess my part in it. My earnings last year – from lectures and conferences alone – exceeded £800,000. This takes no account of the other income I have enjoyed from other crop circle business including well over a quarter of a million pounds from the T-shirt cartel. The cabal of lecturers, writers and photographers all share business managers, personal trainers, hairdressers and tax consultants. Despite PR to the contrary I live in a palatial home by the Mediterranean, returning to Wiltshire in my private jet only when absolutely necessary.

3. Glickman's illness has affected his brain.

It is true, but I have been trying hard to conceal it. Can you just give me a few more minutes before you put on the restraints and take me back to my cell?

4. Shopping Matt Williams was a malicious and vindictive act.

Shame on me! Loathsome and spiteful brute that I am. Far from being the mindless vandal that I and others pilloried so mercilessly, he is – and I have always known it – a quiet and spiritual lad who wanted nothing more than the chance to bring the Truth to the world. A chance my selfish actions so cruelly denied him!

5. Michael Glickman and others are cult leaders who will brook no disagreement.

I am guilty as charged. We meet regularly to refine our techniques of subjugation which include sleep-deprivation, mind control through relentless eight hour lectures, religious indoctrination, public humiliations and thumbscrews. Now that we have been exposed, we have decided to break up our cults and release our many victims, like brain-numbed cattle, into the general population. I look back on these and other excesses with shame and horror.

I write these words minutes before I leave for the permanent exile which is now my only option. The car will be here in a moment. Forgive me.

111

2001

There is a tangible satisfaction in living here in Wiltshire in the domain of the circles, and, though I have visited and spent time in the area for many seasons, a close and permanent proximity brings increased awareness. This spring, right on the edge of the 2001 season, various oddnesses and peculiarities have arrived and overlapped. They are portentous.

It takes only a little imagination to recognise that, even before the circles, this was an area of densely layered strangeness. Stone circles and monoliths, barrows and the enormous conical mass of Silbury Hill, white horses, the Wansdyke and the Ridgeway; all of these fold exquisitely into a pattern of hills and woods, valleys and villages which murmur mysteriously of old secrets, of ancient habitation, and, above all, of a rare kind of beauty. Whatever is happening here, it is surely taking place on the most appropriate of enchanted stages.

And then – in this most particular of landscapes – the circles appear. World-views are toppled and lives are changed forever. Marriages break down and others are made. People go mad. Enduring friendships are formed, while earlier ones suddenly become totally irrelevant and are abandoned. Books, magazines, videos, lectures and conferences manifest and disappear, as – equally quickly – do certain people. Pubs & hotels, restaurants & B&Bs lurch from the fashionable to the undesirable and back.

We are all struggling to make sense of this. Some of us work to make our own little brick to add to the communal wall of information, while others view this chaos as little more than a chance to polish their careers or egos.

This contained and lovely area has been selected (By whom? What for?) as the main annual venue for a bewildering, and inexplicably huge display of land-art. The tribe committed to visiting and studying this exhibition is as strange and varied, irritating and charming as any group in history.

* * * * *

The first formation of the 2000 season was the Cherhill triangles in oilseed rape. As I write, we are less than a week from the anniversary of that date and the first tentative little yellow flowers have only just appeared in the fields. The wet spring has delayed things substantially this year.

* * * * *

Foot and Mouth disease, or at least the incomprehensible legislation that has been put in place as a result of it, has brought a transformation. My village stinks of disinfectant. All the gates and pathways bear red warning notices. In certain locations you are asked to drive slowly over soaked matting or straw. Last year's delight at seeing tiny lambs suddenly make vertical leaps as one passed is turned into an aching guilt at their probable imminent death.

The media treat it as a political/economic problem. Nobody

mentions the incalculable burden on the national psyche. How does the group consciousness deal with the awareness of daily slaughter, the horror of the plumes of black smoke over the fields, the image of bulldozers and engineering equipment handling tens of thousands of carcasses? How do we calculate the cost of such an assault to our feelings?

And our tribe is thrust into a kind of limbo. Access to the fields was always questionable. It is possible that many of the farmers – already having a hard time – will treat the formations and those who wish to visit them with bitterness and aggression.

* * * * *

When the vertical 1726 shaft opened up in the top of Silbury Hill in May last year, it was possible to see this as an uncorking of the mysterious earth energy that the hill seems to represent and contain. The unfolding of the crop circle season, the repeated sightings of lights and luminosities and (for me, at least) the reiteration of specific numerological references around the hill supported this view.

Of course, for English Heritage, the nominal caretakers of the monument since it was donated to the nation by Lord Avebury, all this was crankiness and not worthy of the slightest attention. For them, the opening of the shaft was simply the mechanical and entirely explicable result of an unusually wet spring. Why then did they do nothing about it? True, they acted promptly to keep people away in the manner of government and public agencies. Totally ineffectual guards were posted in a small van at the base of the hill to read the papers and smoke for an hour or two, a high wire fence was constructed around the top and a metal lid was built to cover the hole. English Heritage then went into interminable conference with an assortment of historians, curators, archaeologists and engineers. Early in December, the shaft collapsed inwards from the side and since then it has continued to do so. The result is that a vertical hole, about eight feet in diameter and exactly 33 feet deep has eroded further. Soon the area of collapse was bigger than the metal lid, which had to be removed, and a gigantic, unstable bowl was formed at the top of this noble monument. This acts as an efficient funnel to collect rainfall, which it then focuses to saturate the heart of the hill. The size of the crater is such that it is now approaching the edge of the top and threatens to transform the profile forever. Even the local paper, the normally staid *Gazette and Herald*, has expressed its anxiety. English Heritage continues to sit, and whinge, and watch!

This seems to be the worst kind of vandalism by neglect. Silbury Hill will preside wounded over the coming season.

* * * * *

The greatest publicity the crop circle phenomenon has had in years came last summer. Colin Andrews, widely identified as "Dr." Andrews or an "American scientist", pronounced with an air of Mussolini-like certainty that 80% of formations were man-made. His "detective agencies" had proved it and the evidence would be presented in a "paper" which he was producing with "PhDs" and which would be published in a "peer-review" journal later in the year.

Of course, 10 months later, 10 MONTHS, this fraudulent circus has offered no solid support for its fantastic claims and, to be honest, few expected it. Colin Andrews is a skilled practitioner of the "loudest-kid-in-the-playground-wins-the-game" school of discourse and has had many successes by simple and relentless repetition. The real

116

weirdness is this. With barely an iota of evidence, hardly a shred of documentation, without a hint of substantiation, many people actually do believe him!

Fasten your seatbelts. This season could be a bumpy ride...

* * * * *

I want to flip back and remember the The Bishops Cannings Basket which arrived on 6th August 1999 at the end of what had already been an extraordinary season. The development of seven-fold geometry, initiated the previous year, had culminated with the lovely Roundway 'splash' formation which will probably remain the most beautiful seven of all time. The amazing positive/negative square fractals of Windmill Hill and Kennett, the elegantly proportioned star of the Devil's Den, the crescents – swirling at Cherhill and interlocked at Barbury Castle – and the Isometric Cubes of Honeystreet and Allington Down contributed to that awesome year's portfolio.

And yet the Basket, sneaked in towards the end of the season and promptly cut out by an irate farmer, still haunts me as possibly one of the most significant gifts the phenomenon has ever offered.

To understand it fully, we should go back to the Longwood Warren formation of 1995. There has been much excellent work on Longwood Warren, in particular the astronomical analyses by Jack Sullivan, but I want here to concentrate on another single remarkable characteristic. Before Longwood Warren, the crop circle medium was laid crop. The drawing stylus could be imagined as flattening the wheat. But, uniquely, this formation reversed the code. The elegant circles and orbit lines were 'drawn' in thin lines of standing crop in a laid field.

This was the equivalent of changing a drawing protocol from black line on white paper to white line on black paper, but the real technical implications of this are shocking. Perfect circular standing walls, about eight inches wide, were left presiding over a field of flattened wheat. Pause for a moment and consider how difficult this was to achieve.

We had never seen this before and we were not to see it again until the Bishops Cannings Basket, where, again, thin rings, smaller this time, were left standing out of a laid (this time woven!) field. There was much to read geometrically and numerologically, too. Another seven-fold, with each petal formed of four elegantly diminishing rings (28), was joined at the centre by the smallest single ring making a total of the magic 29. Nothing remotely like the basket-weave of the floor had ever been seen before and, while there were a couple of weaves in 2000, they were never again to achieve the Bishops Cannings standard.

The circles avoid competition. To suggest that this formation gave us the best ground-lay ever is somehow distasteful. But it's true!

* * * * *

It took over a year for the unrelentingly implausible Mattie Williams to claim the Bishops Cannings Basket. Of course, there was no supporting evidence. How could there be? It was simply the floating of another lie. Perhaps someone might swallow it.

However, he and some members of his mob were commissioned to make a replica of the Longwood Warren formation for the film *A Place To Stay*. Given that 95% of the problem is design and geometry, subjects in which Williams and team regularly reveal themselves to be below-par, this was a golden opportunity. They had, simply, to replicate a previous formation. How did they do?

The lay was aggressive and mechanical and clearly showed immediate evidence of board marks at a ground level. The original was distinguished by the smooth curvature and precisely even thickness of the wall. They failed miserably here. Look at it and compare. Compare, above all, the internal angles. (Perhaps I am giving something away here, but what the hell! It's about time they learned a few advanced monkey tricks and got themselves out of kindergarten.)

Internal angles are very often what separates the men from the boys, the real from the false, the amateur from the professional. Matthew, look at the way the orbit line joined the planets in the Longwood Warren formation. Sharp, elegant precise. Now look at the same detail in your attempt. Gloopy, like melted wax.

HTV asked me to critique the recent Team Satan Beckhampton formation. I said it was like the over-elaborated busywork of a teenager with a new compass.

After all the claims, boasts and assertions, is this REALLY the best they can do?

* * * * *

The Milk Hill giant arrived on the 12th August. There were 409 circles (a 13 number) in the formation. Each of its six huge arms had thirteen main circles, disposed on a single, simple arc of curvature. The circles increased in size from the first to the seventh and then decreased as they curved away. The seventh, largest circle – about 72 feet in diameter – was also the point of junction with the neighbouring arm. There were six of these and they were the same size as the central mother circle, making seven. As each arm curved to join its neighbour at number seven, circle six lost one side of tiny satellite circles to accommodate the junction. If these seven large circles were to be joined by straight lines, they would show six equilateral triangles packed together to form a hexagon.

Like the renowned major formations of 1996, the Stonehenge Julia set, the Alton Barnes DNA and Windmill Hill Triple Spiral, all the arms of circles were developed along a preliminary and continuous tracer path, which, again, was about eight inches wide. This might also be called a hospitality path, for its main function seems to have been the formation of access gateways from circle to circle.

At 780 feet across this was not the largest linear dimension we have had, but it was by far the biggest area ever covered by a crop formation. Apart from this, it might be called a conventional formation. Its design and geometry proposed no new ideas or strategies. It was simply the scale, the raw hugeness, that took the breath away.

I visited it one Thursday morning. There must have been 70 or 80 people inside, but they all seemed so tiny, so far away, dwarfed by the majesty of this thing. After featuring in many of the national daily papers it drew an enormous number of visitors and by the weekend of 1st and 2nd September it had been completely and unrecognisably stomped.

What then might be the significance of Milk Hill? I suggest that this was the huge wax seal at the bottom of a Proclamation. "Claim THIS, you small people!" it said. "Doubt THIS one, faint-hearted ones."

* * * * *

Around the 14th August, the inscrutable Chilbolton Face arrived, followed on the 19th by the Arecibo response. Was there ever a more startling opening? Was there ever a more undeniable sign that things had changed?

The Face gazes at us enigmatically. We are given few clues. Who is this being? Is it male or female? We are stared at through a rectangular frame, ten feet in width on the ground. Is this a window, a picture frame, or perhaps a mirror?

I have suggested often that the veil between dimensions was wearing thin and that the crop circles were events breaking through tears in the cloth. The Chilbolton face looks at us through a woven, and now slightly threadbare, screen of fabric. But perhaps the most arresting characteristic is that we are seeing a rather coarse 'Half-tone'. The Half-tone is a system, invented at the end of the Nineteenth Century by Frederic Eugene Ives, to allow photographic images to be quickly and easily rendered into print. The vast majority of photographic images we see are Half-tones. Take a magnifying glass and look closely at any newspaper photo and you will see that a white, through grey to black, photographic image has been produced entirely by the use of pure black dots (of varying sizes and proximity) on pure white space. Our brain works, within the limits of our visual acuity, to make a smooth, realistic image of the random blobs. And so it is with the Face. But how telling that the opening of this new dialogue starts with the adoption of a technology which, for over a century, has been so fundamental a part of our visual language.

* * * * *

The original SETI transmission was blasted into the universe from the Arecibo radio telescope in 1974. The scientists, as always confusing the limits of their own imagination with the limits of the universe, assumed that it would take twenty thousand light years to reach its target, the M13 zone of the Milky Way. The response took twenty-seven years! There are many possible reasons for this speedy reply but I offer three.

First, and, of course, much favoured by SETI and others desperate to maintain calm in a rapidly changing world: The Chilbolton events are a hoax, or as SETI prefers, a "prank".

Second: The recipient was merely thirteen and a half light years away (oops, not twenty thousand!) and the reply was sent by return of mail.

Third, and my personal favourite: Our cousins live outside our earthly time constraints and not only did they get the original transmission immediately, they probably understood what it would say before it was dispatched. It was returned to us NOW because, within the trajectory of the evolving crop circle programme, we need it NOW. It is – emphatically – not a "message". It is another piece of a continuing conversation.

Think about it! This is what we are expected to do.

2002

The season approaches and, as always, the murmuring of croppies pawing at the earth, straining at the leash and chomping at the bit increases in volume. Whatever else might be said of this most moving of phenomena, it must be admitted that it produces overwhelming anticipation. Perhaps it's no more than its seasonality.

Meanwhile, I find this spring, like many others, I am assailed with letters, emails and telephone calls seeking answers and information. Most people want to hear how the crops are growing, how the fields look and what stage we are at.

I write this at the beginning of April. We have had a warm spell for a few days and, in the sun, it is impossible not to sense that the winter is tangibly over. The Alton Barnes White Horse looks down friskily from Milk Hill onto the fields that have held so many formations. Driving by it every few days through the changes of season, it serves as a huge marker on the hillside. It shifts in winter from a grey so dark it hardly stands out from the surrounding land, to an increasing whiteness that comes when the air warms and dries the chalk. It is whiter now.

There are hundreds of lambs. After the mishandled horrors of 2001, they are a real reassurance. They deal well with the cold, though rain and wind kills them by the dozen. But there is a sting in the tail of the mild weather. Robust harvest predictions across the country have already depressed future wheat and barley prices. Milk payments to farmers seem also to be dropping (who knows why?). The farmers are nervous about economic pressures.

Wheat and barley are tall enough now for the fields to distinctly reveal the tramlines. The oilseed rape has just started to blossom, and though we have not yet got the brilliant gold carpets, they are clearly on the way. The rape stems are about a foot high and, now that they have flowered, they will grow at an astonishing twelve inches a week. Expect formations in the third week of April.

* * * * *

American schoolchildren with crop circle projects still want to know about Doug and Dave and their self-proclaimed disciples. I remember George Braque's having said "Truth exists. Lies are invented", and always answer them kindly. I explain that, while there are occasional frauds they are very few and are pathetically easy to spot. If they are truly interested in the subject, I advise them to remember to hold the First Axiom close – everything ever stated about hoaxes is a falsehood.

They also ask, usually with excitement, what I think the film *Signs* will do for us. I tell them that the director, M. Night Shyamalan, and the star, Mel Gibson, have both made their lack of interest in the realities of the crop circles radiantly clear. It was inevitable that the Hollywood sausage machine would eventually mince the phenomenon. Many starry-eyed opportunists have tried to hitch their career wagons to the irrelevant *Signs* horse. I foresee the undignified spectacle of their running for cover (excuses ablaze) once the film is released in all its trivial and melodramatic glory.

126

* * * * *

Luminosities seem to play a crucial role in the inception, if not the actual manufacture, of crop circles. In the Oliver's Castle video the first of the two pairs which looped over the field seemed to trigger the construction of the shape, while the second appeared simply to be inspecting it.

Let me list certain events of the past few years which, though proving nothing, might help to paint a clearer picture. With the exception of Barbury Castle 1999, they all took place before, during or very shortly after the arrival of a crop circle.

On the night of 7th August 1997, a party of crop circle researchers from the Czech Republic were on top of Milk Hill for a night watch. During the evening they saw a complex dance of light events over the field at the southern foot of Milk Hill. In the morning, the 8th, the Milk Hill Koch fractal formation had appeared. This was distinguished from the earlier Silbury Koch fractal only by the fact that the Milk Hill formation had a central "rosette". This rosette could be seen as an inwardly operating Koch progression (starting from a hexagon), rather than the outwardly growing system which was developed from an equilateral triangle.

On the night of 8th August 1998, Nikki Saville and her brother Andrew stayed on Adam's Grave and witnessed a remarkable show of luminosities. At about 11.25pm they saw two red balls of light. This continued with the appearance of a white ball, which split into three. These were just the opening events in an elaborate performance which continued until after 5.00am. It was a moonlit night and they said that they could see the crop at Tawsmead Copse being flattened. There was a couple from Oxford with them for much of the night. Nikki and Andrew visited the formation at dawn. They believe they were the first to go in.

Two American ladies, neither of whom had been involved with crop circles, spent the same night on Knap Hill. They were hoping for a UFO sighting. Instead they witnessed the same elaborate choreography of multiple luminosities over Tawsmead Copse. Coincidentally, just as the Milk Hill Koch could be seen as the Silbury Koch with a central figure, Tawsmead Copse was similar to the huge East Field formation which had appeared nearby a month earlier. Both were seven-fold geometries.

The 23rd July 1999 Barbury Castle formation of interlaced crescents was set in a field below the Barbury Castle hill, which offered a perfect position for photography and video. About two weeks after the formation appeared, Don Fletcher was on the hill when he saw, and started to film, a bright single luminosity. It quickly moved out of the crop circle and, accelerating to remarkable velocity, sped northward over the countryside. Don was able to capture the whole event.

On the same afternoon, my colleague Patricia Murray visited the site to take photographs. While she worked, she decided to set up her video camera on a tripod locked onto the formation. She had never done this before and did not consider it seriously. Indeed, she did not view the video for several days. What it showed astonished her, for the film had captured ten or twelve luminosities gently entering and leaving the formation and moving around the people sitting there who, like her, saw nothing. It was like a film of a crowded fish-pond.

This example is unusual in several respects. Firstly, it occurred some time after the arrival of the circle. One could not assume that the luminosities played any part in its manufacture. Secondly, while both these pieces of video are important and groundbreaking records, they do not describe any geometric shape or choreography.

In the evening of 22nd July this year, Terry Hall, his wife, daughter and a friend were on Knap Hill. Ironically, Terry had told his friend – who was rather sceptical, that lights were often seen in the area. It was approaching dusk and they walked to the end of the car park to look across East Field. The light was fading, but they could still make out the beautiful nested squares at South Field which had arrived that morning.

As they watched, a luminosity appeared from the south and stopped above the formation. Terry noted that the time was 9.02pm. The light split into four. One went upwards and stopped, one downwards, one to the left and one to the right. Terry said that the lights held still to form a diamond configuration. After two or three minutes, the four lights moved outwards again to form a larger diamond. The lights then went out simultaneously. He was very specific about the quality of the way they were extinguished. It was not like a light being switched off, he felt, but much more like shutters or blinds being closed. He estimated that the whole sequence took somewhere between seven and ten minutes.

I was particularly intrigued by the idea of a small diamond transforming into a larger diamond. I asked him if they might, in fact, have been squares, narrowed by the position and angle of viewing, and he agreed that this might have been so.

Another curious sighting took place on the night of 16th July 2002. Guro Kokaas Parvanova of Norway was standing outside her rented cottage in Manningford Abbots, which is about two miles away from the Pewsey White Horse. She was looking towards the White Horse when she noticed lights. She was astonished that the "lights repeatedly went down into the ground. " She shared the event with colleagues, who were happy to discover the Nautilus formation below the White Horse the next morning.

My impression is that the luminosities are seen in two distinct modes. The first is casual, when they are observed going from place to place or moving around a field or formation and, though enigmatic as ever, exhibiting no particular agenda. The second mode, always associated with a new formation, conforms to a specific procedure, which appears to involve pattern making, colour and ordered movement.

131

2003

Looking back, I realise that, in circles, I, like many others, have often been overwhelmed by a sense of lethargy, lack of focus, loss of memory, a repeated inability to count or do simple sums. In short, befuddlement! Now, the first reaction of any card-carrying earthling (one of which I am) is self-doubt. We have all been exquisitely trained in this for centuries, if not millennia. Why am I so tired? How could I have forgotten that? Were there ten or twelve lines? How could I be so DUMB?

Surveying the Avebury Trusloe Pentagram of 1998, an expert surveyor took a compass reading literally 180° at variance with mine. We both revisited the site, checked our bearings and – four years later – have not reached a conclusion.

There are stories of the total confusion of surveying teams who were unable to reach agreement on a matter as fundamental as the number of elements in a formation. They could not decide whether there were ten or eleven circles. Similarly, people talk of an impenetrable muddle of dimensions: was it 6' 4" or 4' 6"?

The circles seem never to confuse those who enter in order simply to experience and enjoy them. It appears that only those undertaking a rational task are affected. Right-brain intuitive experience is somehow easy (indeed normal) within the circles, while left-brain reasoning activity is somehow difficult.

Perhaps we have stumbled onto an essential component of the crop circle curriculum. Is it possible that we are being encouraged to use and develop our intuition? Maybe a central part of the crop circle course is gently to wean us off our overwhelming dependence on rational, evidence-based enquiry. Perhaps we are being shown that this phenomenon responds more readily to our perception, our consciousness and our IDEAS than to our bean-counting skills.

* * * * *

It is a lovely spring. A couple of days ago I noticed, in Alton Barnes, the first sprinklings of yellow rape flowers. The plants will grow an inch a day through April. Off we go. We are on the brink of another momentous season.

* * * * *

Swirled News from Wiltshire. I have been calling English Heritage to ask if we might expect the cheap metal fence to be removed from the top of Silbury Hill. The summer season will bring thousands of visitors to admire the hill and to marvel at the respect we show for the World Heritage Site of which we are custodians. Since I wrote this paragraph, the engineers and contractors have moved huts and machinery to the base of the hill. Clearly, not only is the fence to stay, but more elaborate and unsightly, and above all unnecessary, operations are to take place.

The Silbury Hill shaft collapsed in May 2000. I write this in June 2003 and – as I reported not long ago – the residue of the repair (over three years later!) is a square of industrial fencing at the top of the hill.

A Crown of Thorns. The noble and elegant silhouette, which has been a presence and reassurance to many thousands over the centuries, is desecrated and vandalised by the very organization which is charged with its custody.

* * * * *

I have been invited to the unveiling of a commemorative plaque on the wall of the London house where lived Joe Slovo and Ruth First. Slovo and First (who was ultimately killed by a letter bomb dispatched to her Mozambique University office by the notorious BOSS) were white South African revolutionaries and members of the ANC in the apartheid years. Slovo became the only white member of the Nelson Mandela government. Mandela himself will be unveiling the plaque.

This forthcoming event has drawn to my attention that commemorative plaques are under the general management of – wait for it – English Heritage! Their "commissioner" is one Loyd Grossman. Now, for non-UK residents I should explain that Loyd Grossman is an American who has become a TV personality in Britain. He has three notable achievements. First (and resulting from a period hosting a cooking show), his face now peers at us from pasta-sauce labels on supermarket shelves, very much in the Paul Newman manner. Second (stick with it), our Loyd presents *Through the Keyhole*, a game in which he wanders around the empty home of a celebrity pointing out furniture, paintings, books and other features of the interior. A team, back in the studio, has to guess – from the style and the possessions – whose house it might be. This is not quite Reality TV, but it is most certainly Voyeur TV. Third, our American cousin Grossman has devised for himself a remarkable and totally invented English accent, rich in tortured vowel sounds and grinding syllables. For many years I laboured under the misapprehension that Dick van Dyke's attempts at Mockney as the chimney-sweep in *Mary Poppins* marked the absolute limit of the possible when it came to truly rotten British accents. I was wrong! English Heritage's very own Grossman takes the prize!.

For a year or two I have laboured under an equally false presumption. I felt that E.H.'s treatment of Silbury marked the zenith of disrespect for our national monuments. How wrong could I be?

* * * * *

When last in London I noticed on the Thames Embankment an imposing bronze bust of the strikingly mustachioed Sir Joseph Bazalgette CB. He was responsible for the design and construction of the London Main Drainage System, a system which operates, largely unaltered, today. As a visionary act of urban engineering, Bazalgette's achievement has been compared with Baron Haussman's construction of the Paris boulevards. Sir Joseph's great-grandson is Peter Bazalgette, the brain behind *Big Brother*. Clearly, a talent for the pumping of sewage runs in the family, for some weeks ago, a series of adverts on Channel 4 TV started promoting the latest series of *Big Brother*. Again, for non-UK residents I should explain that *Big Brother* is a programme with a simple (but hugely popular) premise. A number of people are chosen to be imprisoned in a well-equipped, purpose-built and hermetically-sealed "house". There are banks of cameras in every space, including the bathrooms, and the inhabitants are mercilessly observed for every moment of the day. EVERY moment.

Once a week, the viewing public (which has been gazing fascinated, as though at the behaviour of dysfunctional lab rats) is invited to select the wretched contestant who will be ignominiously rejected and cast back into the real world. This telephone voting earns massive revenue for the producers of the programme. The participants are profoundly unremarkable but there is something almost pornographic in the way we can snoop on their every action. A tabloid newspaper has offered a prize of £50,000 to any contestants who have sex. This is the quintessence of Voyeur TV.

The *Big Brother* logo is a stylized eye, simply constructed with a radial geometry. In the adverts we are shown this logo drawn huge in the sand on a beach, as a crop circle, and finally – shockingly – painted onto the grass right by the Uffington White Horse.

The Uffington horse is the most ancient and most mysterious chalk-carving in Britain. Its custodians are not English Heritage, but an equally feckless organization, the National Trust. There was an outcry when this famous and elegant symbol was used for such a crass commercial purpose. How, people demanded, could the National Trust stoop so low? Well, they replied, we were paid £2000!

Two thousand rotten pounds to allow this marvellous artefact to be hijacked by advertisers!

* * * * *

It has come to my attention that Stonehenge (presented to the nation to by Sir Cecil Chubb with a condition that entrance fee would never be more than one shilling, or 5p) was considered for REMOVAL during the Great War. The 'authorities' (that word again), having constructed what was in those days called an aerodrome at Thruxton, not far from the henge, applied for its demolition as the stones "constituted a dangerous hazard to low-flying aircraft."

There seems to be no limit to the defacement that the authorities are prepared to visit on the precious sites and monuments in their charge. Perhaps, also, it might teach us to beware of those who characterise themselves as "an authority".

* * * * *

I believe the crop circles, in some as yet only faintly understood way, are endeavouring to help us through the shift from the Third to the Fifth Dimension. I see the crop circle community as an air balloon club which has split into two camps. Part of the group is nervous but curious. They want to rise as high as possible into the sky and allow the balloon to take them where it will. The other part is fascinated but too frightened to risk the leap beyond existing reality, beyond the Third Dimension. They will ascend, but only so high and only in balloons firmly tethered to gigantic concrete blocks. The blocks have comforting labels such as "The certainties of scientism", "The comforts of hoaxing" and "Newtonian reality forever!". Firmly anchored to their favourite block (and there are dozens), a safe little jaunt can be experienced. But don't worry! The cable is strong. You won't go up too high or see too far.

* * * * *

You enter the turbulent and unpredictable waters of crop circle studies at your own risk. In fourteen astonishing years I have known many – some of them dear and close friends – who were unable to handle the treacherous currents. Some were swept away and a few were sucked below the surface, never to reappear. Most were simply beached.

As we swim by, they remain standing on the banks, embittered and bewildered, searching to relive the moments before they took the wrong turn.

And, looking back, I see that every accident, every drowning, was simply the result of a lack of discernment.

I do not claim here to be the most discerning person in the world, but I flag it as a goal. The weight of humanness lies as heavily on my shoulders as it lies on yours!

I mention all this because a 'Marshall Masters' has just jumped in and very publicly immersed himself. He disdains discernment. He doggy-paddles like crazy, but clearly finds it hard to swim in these waters.

He posted a piece on the net entitled "Are England's Crop Circles Being Covertly Suppressed?" Marshall Masters puts much emphasis on Linda Moulton Howe's sighting of a helicopter at Lockeridge. He goes to great lengths to give us specification details of the AH-64A/D Apache attack helicopter. He gives us its history and some of its radar and armament capacity. Why exactly? What has this to do with crop circles?

It would have taken little research to discover that, just ten miles south of the main crop circle area is Salisbury Plain, one of the largest military locations in Europe. Several times a month, the windows of my house shake to the reverberations of their artillery practice. Two days ago, returning home from a shopping trip to Marlborough I saw – shock! horror! – a military helicopter!

Masters then says "Now all this brings us to a simple question. Why would anyone use such an impressive armada of technology to harass English farmers and crop circle researchers?"

I live here. I know several local farmers personally. Not one of them believes that they have ever been "harassed" by military technology. As to crop circle researchers, does he believe that Ms. Howe was being personally scanned with the Northrop Grumman millimeter-wave radar for eventual targeting with the Longbow Hellfire missile?

But this brings me to two simple questions of my own. First, why do certain people feel so compelled to publish such fear-based and paranoia-promoting fantasies? Second, why does Masters not follow his own ideas through? If this cover-up notion of his had the slightest validity, the army would be excluding the public from large areas while crop circles were cut out. This has never happened. What part does he imagine helicopters might play in this scenario?

In Southern California girls bathing topless in secluded and private areas often find that LAPD helicopters are hovering overhead to spy on them. Why? Indeed! Perhaps human beings flying over crop circles are similarly intrigued by these inexplicably beautiful formations in the fields.

In my next column I hope to present my thoughts on heart surgery. I know absolutely nothing about it and I certainly will not stoop to take any advice!

* * * * *

A dear friend of mine, a very old lady, has a special relationship with her TV remote. She puts on her spectacles to change channels because she fears that, if she does not aim carefully, she will mark the wall or damage an ornament.

As Robert Downey Jr. so acutely remarked in *Air America*, "No need to give up a good theory just because it isn't true."

I know what he means. For days my house has been shaken (as has the whole area) by the noise of explosions. It is artillery practice time on Salisbury Plain and they seem to have upgraded the shell size. I strongly suspect that the sole purpose of these loud bangs is to irritate me at my desk as I write about the circles.

Animals have four legs. A table has four legs. Therefore a table must be an animal.

142

2004

Here in the Vale of Pewsey, spring arrived, early and unannounced. Before even the middle of February there were days when the sun shone with defiant glee. The weathermen, apparently taking their cue from both British and US fear-promoting governments, issued dire warnings about gales and blizzards.

Accordingly, on hearing the news of an impending meteorological cataclysm, I bought enough food to see me through the equivalent of the Leningrad siege, stuffed my freezer and battened down the metaphorical hatches. The next morning, and indeed the following few days, were sunny and warm. Ah, well. I suppose weather forecasts are just about as reliable as what the authorities see fit to call "intelligence". We have all come to understand the reliability of that.

And then, some time later, there was a little snow! The chalk downs along the northern flank of the Pewsey Vale are magically transformed by snow. The hills seem, for a few hours, to have been lightly dusted with icing sugar.

And now, at the beginning of April, it is definitely spring. Daffodils, a crocus or two, buds on trees, and – above all – burgeoning fields. Touring famous old fields, last year's cerealogical events are still there in silhouette.

* * * * *

Other local news. A drunk driver ran off the A4 into the little Murco garage near Lockeridge. He squarely hit one of the pumps which responded by exploding! There were no injuries, but the car and the petrol station were torched. A familiar landmark in crop circle territory has been destroyed.

Meanwhile, Silbury Hill has been further vandalised by its supposed custodians, English Heritage. They protected the exposed top so inadequately that there was a further collapse some time later, which turned an eight foot diameter hole into a crater. The crater grew and eventually became so large that the edge, and thus the profile of the hill, was threatened.

After an inordinate delay they started remedial work. This involved packing the void with a polystyrene-based foam. Forgive me, but this seems as obscene as packing the human breast with silicone. The construction site at the top of the hill needed to be protected, and accordingly English Heritage did what they do best, they put another fence up on top of the hill.

I accept that I might be prejudiced and over-emotional, but I feel that the spirit of English Heritage delights, above all, in Enclosure and Exclusion. We were told that the plastic filling would be removed eventually. Eventually was never defined. The work finished two years ago, but they could not be bothered to remove the fence.

I contacted English Heritage who, in time-honoured tradition, failed to reply. So I wrote to Lord Avebury, Lord Melchett, Prince Charles, Michael Ancram (the local Member of Parliament) and numerous local councillors.

It got onto Wiltshire Sound radio and, abracadabra, the fence has disappeared. I am pleased (and rather proud) to tell you that the lovely hill is restored.

Next, the plastic stuffing!

* * * * *

More news. A dockyard worker (who wishes to remain anonymous) living in the St. Budeaux area of Plymouth, Devon, bought himself a new digital camera and took a few experimental shots across the rooftops of the town. When he got home to examine the images, he was astonished to discover a gigantic circular object in the sky in several of the pictures. He contacted a local UFO researcher, who had the images checked. They were impeccable and were featured on several pages of the local paper.

Closer to home, there have been several independent sightings of a ring of lights "brighter than the moon" over Pewsey Vale. As the word gets out, more and more people, including a group at Alton Barnes, say that they saw it too.

Closer still to home, you can always be sure that the crop circle season is about to start by the way envy, gossip, vituperation and jealousy start to bubble to the surface. It is as reliable as the whistle that signals the imminent departure of the mail train.

What is it about us earthlings, and crop circle earthlings in particular, that makes us so insecure? How, faced with gifts of miracles, are we so consistently able to dredge the murkiest depths of our character? In the cosmic scheme of things, I imagine we are the prizewinners in the dysfunction stakes. And yes, to pre-empt the inevitable snipes, I do include myself here.

Nancy Talbott recently announced what seemed to be very positive results from her and Doctors Burke and Levengood's work on soil analysis from crop circles conducted in the US. It seems there is a measurable change in the soil as well as in the crops themselves. I called her in Cambridge to thank her and congratulate her, though, as a non-scientist, I admit only a superficial understanding of the work.

Within days the internet was on fire!

A famous researcher pitched in, attempting to hitch his creaky old wagon to the new horse. It was clear he understood even less than I did, but was desperate to get some of the credit. Astonishingly, attempts were made to revive the long-dead 80%/20% corpse. Another pretender to scientific respectability promptly piped up with a pompous criticism of the "methodology" (new failed-croppie buzzword) of the research. I was sent a copy of *The Circular*, a hoax-fancying magazine I had not read for some years. There was a piece attributing to me words which I never said. Is it worth the trouble of replying? Their circulation, apparently, is 17. And, finally, more emails whinging about "rumours".

Here we are, faced with the most extraordinary miracles in the world, and we behave like teenagers in the dormitory. Years ago, I guess I might have been upset. Now, with the prospect of a lovely season ahead, I shrug ruefully.

* * * * *

"Forget, for a moment, the crop circle phenomenon itself. Its effects

146

on its students have produced, virtually unremarked, a soap opera, a Russian novel, a veritable Encyclopaedia Britannica of psycho-social studies." Ofmil C. Haynes at the 1994 Crop Circle Winter Colloquium, Glastonbury.

Ofmil, who died in 1998, did not live to see just how prescient, how prophetic was this remark. Had he lived he would have observed, as the '90s ended, the development of a terrible, and I believe, unbridgeable rift in the crop circle community. The seeds of breakdown were sown by the Doug and Dave fraud of 1991 but have been nurtured by prejudice, fear, untruth and simple stupidity as the years have passed. The 2004 season marked the bleakest moment in this trajectory.

And yet it leaves us all with an obligation to consider more deeply, to bring more wisdom to our understanding and, perhaps, to forgive the fearful, indeed, the terrorised, more comprehensively. We are experiencing, as never before, the miraculous on earth and each of us responds as best we can.

* * * * *

I offer here a breakdown of the crop circle community into its three major components. These ideas are perhaps simplistic and over-reflective of my own prejudices. For this, forgive me. However I hope it might suggest, in troubled times, a basis for discussion.

The A Type Croppie is often called a "believer", though called that only pejoratively, to imply that he or she is a soft-minded sap, a bliss bunny, a New Age crystal fairy who will accept anything. The truth is very different. The A Type is both bewildered and delighted by the crop circles. The A Type holds no firm idea as to where they might come from, who is causing them or what they might mean. While the A Type will continue to speculate and take pleasure in ideas and conjectures, it is the B Type who loudly trumpets the certainties of his inevitably unsupported and unsupportable "solutions", "explanations" or, more regularly percentages.

Perhaps A Types started by pursuing the elusive "explanation" but soon understood the impossibility of this quest; they remain, now, comfortable with the experience of the ineffable unknown, content with suppositions and hypotheses, at ease, simply, with the journey, though towards what remains questionable. They have long lost their desperation to explain or categorise.

A Types are open and happy individuals who regard the crop circles as a doorway to evolution and expansion, They are friendly and optimistic. They are honest and are always prepared to share their views, their work and their research. I have never known an A Type to be secretive.

They find the mysterious and inexplicable seductive, and it holds no terror for them.

The majority of B Type Croppies were once A Types and are predominantly male. Depending on your position, the B might be called a Lapsed or Recovering A. They have an overwhelming air of disappointment, a sense that they were, in some unidentifiable way, let down or cheated by the phenomenon. They always hoped the circles would conform to a conventional framework of belief. When the phenomenon resisted a simple (and preferably a "scientific") explanation, the B's reached – like drowning men – for the "total hoax theory", now expanded to encompass the absurd "land art" position. They often look back with nostalgia to the mythical "good old days" of the late '80s and early '90, the simple and undemanding circles and rings.

While continuing to deride the soft-minded A, they occasionally arrive at conferences, their eyes telegraphing anxiety and depression. The B Type is the true "Believer" for they have created an unquestionable fundamentalism. "All crop circles are man-made!" they declare with conviction "Or if not all, then certainly most. Anyway, a lot. And I met someone in the pub who told me. . . "

B Types do not have much fun. They accuse A's of being "popular" or "making money". Their bitterness towards those who have retained what they themselves once had (but chose to jettison) is tangible. Having renounced their open bewilderment in the inexplicable, they are envious at the ease with which A's swim in these waters.

B's are aware, above all, of the need for good citizenship, and shudder to challenge conventional wisdom. At heart, fascinated as they might be by the crop circles, they fear social disapproval.

The C Type is best-known as the "hoaxer". Many hoaxers, like B's, are in fact ex-A's who, generally now, they despise. Obsessed with deception, their greatest pleasure is the discomfiture of others. Like B's much of their drive comes from envy and bitterness. When challenged about their secrecy and refusal to participate, they will always whine that, whenever they have tried to communicate with A-types, they are met with cynicism and disbelief.

Some years ago their strategy shifted. While never for a moment ceasing to lambast every A as deluded, they suddenly started to claim profound mystical experiences around the circles. Thus, we have now achieved the ultimate absurdity. The circles, they claim, are no more than "land art" made by "human circle facilitators" and yet the very moment hoax teams enter the fields, they are miraculously blessed with the ability to be in touch with the numinous and spiritual which, by definition, can only be accessed by them.

* * * * *

In an age where the truest and scariest fundamentalism is Scientism, it is risky to defy the authority of science. But we all know that we are living in an all-pervasive cloud of the mysterious and the inexplicable. The job of Scientism (and its priests are given status for handling this) is to "explain" that which it can understand and quantify and to simply exclude the inexplicable and the unquantifiable from the consensus. The corridors of science are "exclusive" because they so efficiently exclude.

To step outside the consensus is to venture into the void. There are no rules. The bets are off and you will almost certainly be sneered at and abused.

2005

The 2005 season and its aftermath will be remembered for two momentous events: the Centre for Crop Circles Studies' decision to close itself down, and later, Colin Andrews' offer for sale of his archive, signalling in effect his decision also to close himself down.

Neither of these items will come as much of a surprise to seasoned circle-watchers. Both the CCCS and Andrews have been labouring for years under the unbearable weight of their private delusions. Their distance from (and indeed their lack of true interest in) the crop circle phenomenon have been among the more remarkable sideshows of recent years.

I look at both these events with real sadness and overwhelming pity. Illusions shattered, dreams unrealised, boats missed. Those of us who are close to this phenomenon have been blessed in our lifetime by glimpses of the miraculous. I can imagine no greater torment than being closely involved and yet deciding to miss the point.

But, sorry as I am for the CCCS, whose council members truly felt they were doing their best, I am relieved, finally, that it has gone. I have had the sense over the last year that we all need to do our spring cleaning and black bagging.

New furniture is required. I am always heartened by the arrival, year by year, of new blood, young people and fresh ideas.

* * * * *

As we go to press, the internet is alive with rumours that Nicolas
Cage has sent his people to find a house in either Glastonbury or the
Pewsey Vale. The circles inevitably worked their enigmatic magic on
his subconscious after all. Cage, apparently unable to bear the deep
psychological sense of loss he suffered for years after leaving the
calendar in the cafe, entered a deep course of hypnotic regression. The
images of conferences and symposia, of calendars and yearbooks and,
above all, of crop circles, made him decide to shrug off Hollywood and
make his future here with us.

He has persuaded several other stars to come with him. I am sure
you could not possibly expect me to divulge their names. Anyway, you
will meet them all next season ...